THE ST. LOUIS CARDINALS

MEMORIES AND
MEMORABILIA
FROM A CENTURY
OF BASEBALL

Text by Bruce Chadwick
Photography by David M. Spindel

ABBEVILLE PRESS · PUBLISHERS
New York · London · Paris

To Margie and Rory.
—B.C.

For all the players who played for the love of the game.
—D.M.S.

EDITOR: Stephen Brewer
DESIGNERS: Barbara Balch and Patricia Fabricant
PRODUCTION EDITOR: Owen Dugan
PICTURE EDITOR: Kim Sullivan
PRODUCTION MANAGER: Lou Bilka

Library of Congress Cataloging-in-Publication Data
    Chadwick, Bruce.
        St. Louis Cardinals: memories and memorabilia from a century of baseball/ text by Bruce Chadwick: photography by David Spindel.
            p. cm.
        Includes bibliographical references and index.
        ISBN 1-55859-861-8
        1. St. Louis Cardinals (Baseball team)—History. 2. St. Louis Cardinals (Baseball team)—Collectibles. I. Title.
    GV875.S3C43   1995
    796.357'64'0977866—dc20   91-32027

Pages 2–3:
The St. Louis Cardinals were poised to do great things by the end of the 1920s (see p. 34).
Frontispiece:
A bounty of Cardinals memorabilia.
Title page: Official proof of Knot Hole

Gang membership (see p. 40) and a ball with Dizzy Dean's autograph (see p. 54).
This page:
A pin from 1942 Series, one of three the Cards won during the decade (see p. 65).

Page 7: A piece of contemporary memorabilia (see. p. 112).
Pages 8–9: Ticket stubs from the 1926 Series (see. p. 35); a Cards–Coca-Cola pin (see p. 131); a Stan Musial pin (see p. 90); the Deans as hucksters (see p. 53);

a familiar sign (see p. 111) a Cards bottle (see p. 119); 1950s memorabilia (see p. 83); the 1913 schedule on a coin (see p. 24).

ACKNOWLEDGMENTS

We'd like to thank the staff of the St. Louis Cardinals, particularly Marty Hendin and Jeff Wehling, for all their help and cooperation on this book. We're also grateful to Paula Homan, curator of the Cardinals Hall of Fame, and Hall of Fame historian Erv Fischer for helping us photograph memorabilia there. Thanks, too, to the staff at the National Baseball Hall of Fame in Cooperstown, New York, particularly the director of its photo archives, Patricia Kelly. Finally, special thanks to our editor, Stephen Brewer, and designers Patricia Fabricant and Barbara Balch, who worked with us on the book.

BRUCE CHADWICK AND DAVID M. SPINDEL

CONTENTS

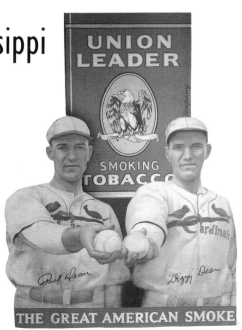

PENNANTS AND MEMORIES

arge, bright red banners celebrating each of the St. Louis Cardinals' pennants and world championships hang from the ceiling of the concourse behind home plate at Busch Stadium. The Cards have won so many championships and world titles that these banners form an almost endless wave of cardinal red as far as the eye can see.

Actually, these flags don't even represent all the titles Saint Louis baseball teams have won over the years. Saint Louis won a number of pennants way back in the 1880s, when the Cardinals' forebears, the Browns, played in the old American Association. A Saint Louis team, the Maroons, was a member of the National League in its first season, in 1876. Along the way, the other Browns, of the American League, made Saint Louis a two-baseball-team town for the first half of this century. The Stars, of the Negro League, also drew large crowds. But it is the Cardinals, with all those flags and all those heroes, who have dominated baseball in this baseball city.

The Cards have won sixteen pennants and nine world championships in their many years in the National League. They have played in two of baseball's most memorable stadiums, Sportsman's Park, where the stands were so close to the field fans felt they were a part of the game, and Busch Stadium, a catalyst for the redevelopment of the entire downtown

Bright banners hanging at **Busch Stadium** capture the glory of one of baseball's greatest teams.

These tags celebrate the great players of Cardinals history.

area when it opened in 1966. The Cardinals have made history in both these parks and in the parks in which they played in the 19th century, and they have given the game some of its most colorful characters and greatest heroes. The Cards' first owner, barrel-chested, flamboyant Chris Von Der Ahe, was a circus-style promoter who used an all-female band and other promotions to get fans into the ballpark. Branch Rickey, who took over the reins in

the 1920s, developed a vast minor-league farm system, which kept the Cards on top for decades.

Then, of course, there are the players: Ozzie Smith, Joe Torre, Curt Flood, Lou Brock, Bob Gibson, Red Schoendienst, Johnny Mize, Ken Boyer, Stan Musial, and Rogers Hornsby, to name only some of the greats who have played for the Cardinals over the years. The boys of the Gashouse Gang of the 1930s—Dizzy Dean and his brother Daffy, Ducky Medwick, Pepper Martin, Lon Warneke, Frankie Frisch, and Leo Durocher—not only brought the Cards two world championships and three pennants, but delighted fans with their antics.

Looking back over more recent history, who can forget Enos Slaughter's race from first to home in the final inning of the 1946 World Series? How a team of fiery players in the 1960s, led by Bob ("the plate is mine") Gibson, Curt Flood, and Lou Brock, brought the team back to the top

after doldrums in the 1950s to win two world titles and three pennants? Or the pigeon-toed stance and innocent charm of the great Stan Musial? Or manager Whitey Herzog and his speed, speed, speed offense that in the 1980s once again brought world championships to Saint Louis, with talented players such as Ozzie Smith, Willie McGee, Tommy Herr, Vince Coleman, Bob Forsch, and John Tudor.

These athletes have given Saint Louis a century of great baseball—and a century of great memories.

Catcher's gear of a bygone era evokes all the romance of the game.

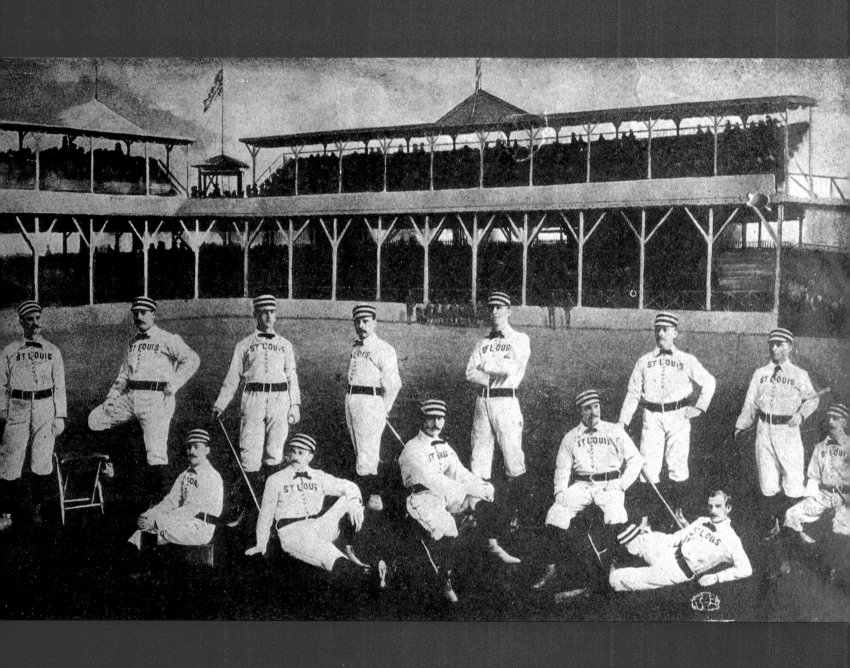

BASEBALL ON THE MISSISSIPPI
1876–1916

Saint Louis was exploding in 1882. The population of the city, which included thousands of immigrants and a broad, blue-collar middle class, had more than doubled in twenty years, to 360,000 people. It was one of America's busiest port cities, the hub to fifteen of the largest railroads in the country, and the jumping-off point for the streams of pioneers and families headed west to the wide-open plains and California. A busy and cosmopolitan city with museums, theaters, and annual fairs that were known all over the world, Saint Louis was, in short, an ideal place for a major-league baseball team.

Actually, by then Saint Louis had already fielded a baseball team—the St. Louis Brown Stockings, one of the eight teams in the National League when it debuted in the spring of 1876 (the Stockings had played one year in the old National Association of Professional Base Ball Players in 1875, too.) The 1876 squad finished second to the Chicago White Stockings and included one of the best pitchers of the era, George Washington "No Hit" Bradley, who tossed the first no-hitter in major-league history that summer against Hartford, Connecticut. The club finished fourth in 1877. Hopes were high for a pennant in 1878 after owner John Lucas inked four of the top players from Louisville, Kentucky, which had almost won the pennant in the 1877 season. Then, just before the season

In 1884, the Saint Louis Browns had a new manager—Charles Comiskey (standing, third from right), who would soon turn the team around and become a baseball legend himself.

15

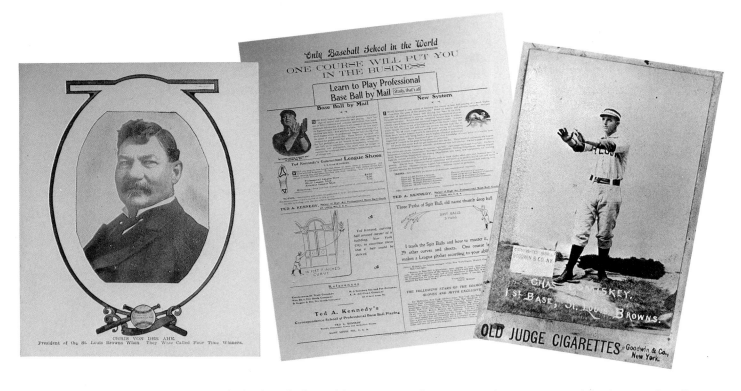

Chris Von Der Ahe, left, flamboyant brewer and owner of the Browns in the 1880s, was as interested in beer sales at Sportsman's Park as he was in the score.

Browns catcher Ted Kennedy ran a baseball correspondence school.

Comiskey earned his greatest fame with the Chicago White Sox, but as player-manager he led the Browns to four straight league titles.

started, the baseball world was stunned when all four players were booted out of the game for allegedly fixing the last few games of the 1877 season, allowing Boston to take the pennant. Soon people were accusing the innocent Lucas of having known about the fix and signing the players anyway. Deluged with accusations and dreadful publicity, he threw up his hands, and pulled his team out of the league.

When the American Association began play in 1882 as the country's second major league, one of its first moves was to grant Chris Von Der Ahe, an eccentric local businessman, its Saint Louis franchise. Von Der Ahe's team, the Browns, would

soon become one of the best and well-known squads in baseball, and Von Der Ahe, who owned blocks of apartment houses and several beer gardens in bawdy, wide-open Saint Louis, would become one of the great characters in baseball history, the George Steinbrenner of his time. He was a tall, heavyset, garrulous man with a bulbous nose who always wore his trademark stovepipe hat, flashy waistcoats, and diamond stickpins in his ties. He was a ladies' man, and the *Sporting News* once ran a cartoon of him with two women on his arm, marching down a street.

Unlike the rival National League, the American Association permitted the sale

These pants, bat, and glove belonged to pitcher Ted Kennedy.

of beer—and Von Der Ahe reasoned that baseball was not only a perfect way to not gather eight-thousand or more people in a spot where he sold beer, but a game in the hot sun would make all those people thirsty. The fans had a demand and he had a supply. Sportsman's Park at Grand Avenue and Dodier Street (later the site of the park of the same name where the Cards would play until the 1960s) was

laced with beer stands, concession booths, and picnic tables. Tickets to the ballgame cost a quarter, and a mug of beer cost a nickel. Saint Louis fans joked that the Browns were "built around a keg of beer and a barrel of pretzels." Von Der Ahe saw his baseball team as an attraction, like the circus, in addition to being a magnet for beer drinkers. Instead of having his players travel from their hotel to the park in enclosed horse cars, for instance, he had them ride in large, open-air carriages. The horses that drew them wore richly colored "St. Louis Browns" blankets.

The beer was tasty and such sideshow attractions were amusing, but the fans really came to the park to see the Browns and the white-hot baseball they played. (The team held its own against a rival, the Maroons, that came to town in 1884 with the Union Association, which went under after one season, then was absorbed by the National League for two more seasons of play before it, too, folded.) Von Der Ahe, who knew next to nothing about baseball, took the advice of friends and hired an unknown sandlot ballplayer named Charley Comiskey as player-manager and first baseman. Young Comiskey was a pioneer (he was the first to play first base six feet off the bag), a shrewd manager, and a good judge of talent, and he turned the Browns into one of the top

17

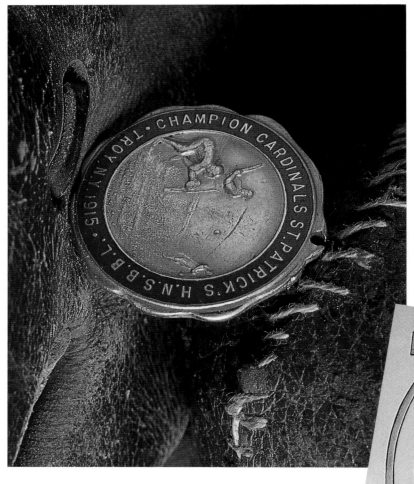

teams of the 1880s. Between 1885 and 1888 they won the American Association pennant four years in a row, won a world championship, in 1886, and tied another in 1885.

Comiskey had some fine hitters, among them Arlie Latham and Tip O'Neill, who hit .435 in 1887, and on the mound he had Bob Caruthers and Dan Foutz. In the 1885, 1886, and 1887 seasons, Caruthers and Foutz each won ninety-nine games. The 1885 and 1886 World Series were wild affairs. The 1885 series against the Chicago White Stockings was halted

One of the many medallions honoring the Cardinals' early triumphs. Stanley Robison, right, came to town from Cleveland in 1899 and took over the Browns.

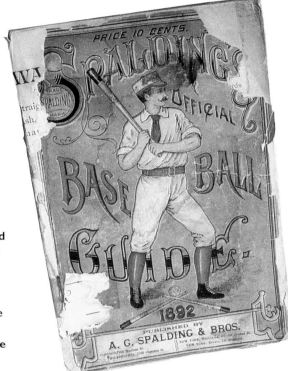

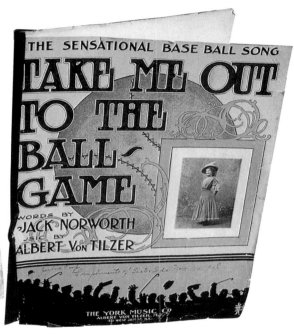

The Browns figured prominently in the Spalding guide of 1892, the year the famous champs became part of the National League. As baseball became more popular, so did the Cards.

after a riot broke out between the players during the seventh game. Cap Anson, player-manager of the White Stockings, was so angry about the resulting tie that when both teams met in the Series again the next year, he refused to play unless they agreed that, breaking with standard procedure, the winners would take all and the losers would take none of the purse. Comiskey and Von Der Ahe agreed. In the final inning of the sixth game, Browns outfielder Curt Welch stole home in one of the most dramatic plays in baseball his-

tory, and the Browns won the game and the Series, four games to two. The Browns pocketed every nickel of the $15,000 purse, and Comiskey and Von Der Ahe made $500 more on bets they made with Anson. When Von Der Ahe heard that many Chicago players had gone bankrupt betting hundreds of dollars on their team, he went to Chicago and gave the losers several thousand dollars out of his own pocket.

Looking to make quick money on the team's success, at the end of the season

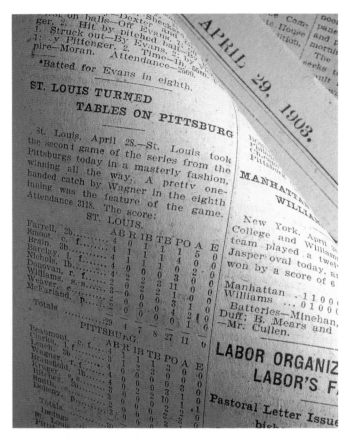

By 1893, the Browns had lost their star power and, despite occasional wins, were slipping.

ican Association to form the Players League. Although there was no Players team in Saint Louis, the Browns lost Comiskey to the Players team in Chicago. The league folded after one season, but caused irreparable damage to the American Association, which folded at the end of the 1891 season. Four of its strongest teams, including Saint Louis, were absorbed into the National League for the 1892 season.

The plunge into the National League was not a happy one for the Browns. Von Der Ahe moved them to a new, larger stadium, League Park, at Vandeventer and Natural Bridge avenues, and in keeping with his usual style, turned it into an amusement park. There was a chute-the-chute ride for kids over the center-field fence, a horse track around the perimeter of the field, a man-made lake on the grounds for boat races, and a wide selection of sideshows to accompany the games, including Wild West shows, boxing matches, and concerts by the Silver Cornets, an all-woman band intended to draw men into the ballpark.

Despite these antics, Von Der Ahe had lost the soul of his lineup and, now that he was in the National League, was faced with teams that were much better than his. The Browns stumbled the first week of the 1892 season and never regained their balance, finishing eleventh in

Von Der Ahe sold Bob Caruthers, Dan Foutz, Curt Welch, and some other players for $15,000. Despite the loss of star power, Comiskey managed to win another pennant in 1888, but the core of his team was gone. In 1889 the Browns slipped to second, and in 1890, everything started to fall apart. That year hundreds of ballplayers, unhappy with their salaries, bolted teams in both the National League and the Amer-

Ted Kennedy was a pioneer in exploiting baseball's wide commercial appeal— his signature gloves were popular with amateurs across the country for decades.

Bugs Raymond was a great pitcher—and a great drinker, too.

a field of twelve teams. Not knowing what to do, Von Der Ahe began firing managers, hiring and firing as many as six a season. The team hovered near the cellar of the league every year of the 1890s.

In the middle of a game in 1898, a fire broke out in the stands, and hundreds of people were burned or trampled in the ensuing panic. The fire destroyed the bleachers, grandstand, clubhouse, offices, and Von Der Ahe's saloon next door. The game was finished the next day, only because Von Der Ahe ordered his ballplayers to help local workers clean up the park and erect four-thousand seats he borrowed from a circus. The Browns finished last that season, and it was Von Der Ahe's last season, too. Faced with dozens of lawsuits, he sold the club to a local lawyer

who, with the league's blessing, sold it to the Robison brothers of Cleveland.

The Robisons moved their team, the Spiders, to Saint Louis in 1899, and renamed it the Browns. The transplanted Cleveland boys were a wild bunch who constantly got into fights, on and off the field, baited umpires mercilessly, and had the rare knack of getting fans to join them in their wars against the umpires. Fans became so enraged with ump Hank O'Day during a game in 1899 that they leaped on to the field and chased him into the clubhouse, where he was rescued by policemen with drawn revolvers. Amid the fights, arguments, and fifth-place finish, the new Browns became the St. Louis Cardinals during that first season of play. To distinguish the players from the old Browns, the

Baseball-related give-aways were wildly popular around the turn of the century.

Roger Bresnahan, a famous catcher and equally famous nightclub hopper, came to the Cards as a player-manager.

owners had them wear bright red socks and red fringe on their uniforms. A local sportswriter, Willie McHale, started calling them the Cardinals, and the name stuck.

Those Cardinals didn't fly very well, however. The team had the league batting champ, Jesse Burkett (with a .402 average one season), but little else. The newly formed American League put a club in Saint Louis in 1902. First the team stole the Cards' old nickname, the Browns, then it stole five of their starting nine and three of their best pitchers. The weakened and depleted Cards managed to finish fourth in 1902, but did not finish that high again for thirteen years. The ball club did have its share of characters, though. One was Bugs Raymond, nicknamed for his bulging eyes. He was a great pitcher and an even greater drinker. He would often show up half soused for a game. He was the bane of president John McCloskey's existence. When Raymond telephoned just fifteen minutes before a 1908 game to say he couldn't pitch because he had a "tooth-ache," McCloskey told him he would be fired if he didn't show up. Bugs, clearly drunk, showed up, took the ball, wobbled to the mound, blinked his red eyes a few times, and beat Chicago, 3–1. Pitcher "Slim" Sallee kept odd hours to pursue his hobby, which was helping Saint Louis milk-men deliver milk. He would stay awake all

From 1911 to 1914, hurler Slim Sallee won at least fifteen games a season for Saint Louis. The odd-ball pitcher's hobby was helping local milkmen make their rounds.

night, make his morning rounds, then sleep until noon. Right fielder Louis Evans was afraid of being badly sunburned, so he played right field very deep so he could stand in the shade of the grandstand. One day, three flyballs fell well in front of him, and the manager ordered him to leave the shade and play closer to the infield. The next inning, Evans ran out into the sunlit outfield and assumed his position, holding an umbrella over his head.

Nothing worked for the Cardinals. Managers came and went. Owner Stanley Robison even hired his concession-stand director to be manager one season. When Robison died in 1911, his niece, Helene Britton, took over. "Lady Bee," as she was called, got rid of then-manager Roger Bresnahan, the nightclub-hopping, former New York catcher, and hired Miller Huggins. He managed to edge the Cards up to third in 1914, but they plunged to sixth the

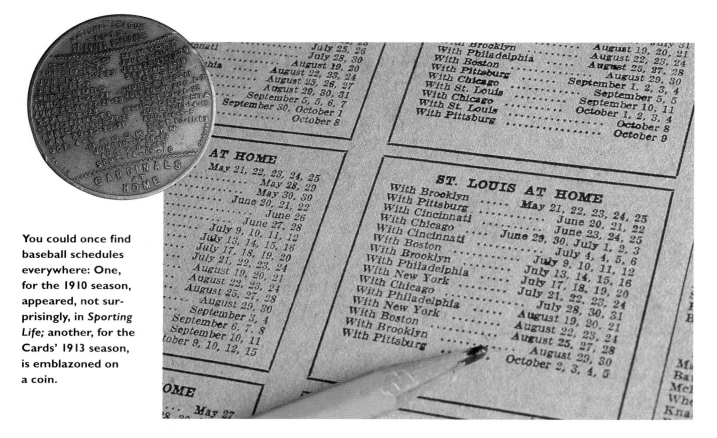

You could once find baseball schedules everywhere: One, for the 1910 season, appeared, not surprisingly, in *Sporting Life*; another, for the Cards' 1913 season, is emblazoned on a coin.

In 1911, Helene Britton became the first woman to own a major-league base-ball team when she inherited the Cardi-nals from her uncle, Stanley Robison.

The Cards were a sound investment.

next year. In the 1914 and 1915 seasons, Britton not only had to go head to head against the American League Browns for fans, but she also had to fight off the new Federal League, which put a franchise, the Miners, in Saint Louis.

After four years at the helm as base-ball's first female executive, in the winter of 1916 Britton sold the Cardinals to local attorney James Jones. Aware that he needed new marketing schemes to build up attendance, Jones was the first executive to organize a knothole gang, a club that let kids into games cheaply in order to develop them as future fans. He also knew he needed a brand-new base-ball man to run the Cardinals. In January 1917, on a cold day when a biting wind whipped through Saint Louis, he met with seven local sportswriters and asked for suggestions. They voted immediately and unanimously: Branch Rickey.

CHAPTER TWO

TO THE TOP
1917–1929

Branch Rickey was unlike any other baseball man of his time. In a world of minimally educated, rough-hewn ballplayers, he was a college professor and held a law degree. In an era when the ballpark was considered to be a place where crude people congregated, Rickey was a Sunday School teacher. While casual dress was the order of the day in baseball circles, Rickey was always dressed elegantly, shoes shined, his trademark bow tie perfectly in place, his hair slicked back.

In 1917 Rickey, who had been a catcher for several minor-league teams and, briefly, for the Yankees, was in limbo. He had managed the American League's St. Louis Browns for several years, but was kicked upstairs as business manager when Phil Ball bought the team. When the Cardinals asked Rickey to be club president, he was glad to go. The Cards finished third in 1917, with Rickey in the front office and Miller Huggins managing in the dugout. When Huggins left to become skipper of the Yankees in 1918, Rickey moved into the dugout to manage the team on the field, and local businessman Sam Breadon reorganized the destitute team and became club president. Rickey and Breadon were social opposites, but Rickey respected Breadon's business sense and Breadon respected Rickey's vision. The biggest part of that vision was developing young talent. At the time, most of the country's 150-some

More than a million citizens of Saint Louis came out to welcome the Cardinals home after they grabbed the 1926 World Series over the New York Yankees.

27

Rickey knew he couldn't outbid the rich teams, so he decided to buy his own minor-league teams and grow his own pitchers and sluggers. It was a daring move, but Breadon backed him. The Cards bought up interest in six minor-league teams in 1920, and by 1940, they would own controlling interest in thirty-three minor-league teams (they owned 100 percent interest in fifteen of them). Rickey even bought up two entire leagues in the 1930s, the Nebraska State League and the Arkansas-Missouri League, though baseball Commissioner Kenesaw Mountain Landis charged the Cards with building a monopoly and ordered the Cards to sell off the teams. The Cards' huge network of teams, which stretched from the West Coast (Sacramento, California, gave the Cards their greatest player of the 1930s, Pepper Martin) to the East Coast (Daytona Beach, Florida, produced hundreds of major-league ballplayers).

To save money, Breadon streamlined the Cardinals' front office, chopping the number of directors from thirty-two to five. He entered a joint-leasing agreement at Sportsman's Park with the Browns, and used the money from the sale of Robison Field (the Robison brothers had so named League Park) to invest in minor-league clubs. He gave Rickey a free hand as manager of the Cards. Through sheer luck,

Branch Rickey was named Cards skipper in 1919 and soon developed an enormous and amazingly productive farm-team system.

minor-league teams were independent and covered their budgets by selling their best players to major-league clubs. The rich teams, like the Giants and Yankees, got the good ones. The poor teams, like the Cards, got the bad ones.

This watch fob and attached knife belonged to Sam Breadon, president of the Cards in the 1920s.

Wearing the caps and swinging the bats of the era, the 1920s Cardinals roared toward greatness.

in 1915 the Cardinals found a kid named Rogers Hornsby. A shortstop turned second baseman, Hornsby, with his storybook swing, hit .313 in 1916, his first full season. In 1920 he hit .370 to lead the league, then led the league for the next five consecutive years, hitting over .400 three times (.424 in 1924). The square-jawed right-hander, who stood deep in the batter's box to get

an extra millisecond on the pitcher, was able to spray hits to any field and hit 289 lifetime homers. He rarely fell into a slump. The phenomenal hitter had a grating personality, however, and could get along with no one. He was constantly fighting with other players and Rickey. An eccentric as well, he told sportswriters he never read the newspapers or went to the movies for

GENUINE
BABY DOLL JACOBSON
LOUISVILLE SLUGGER

Graced with a powerful, flat swing and remarkable hand-eye coordination, Rogers Hornsby was one of the greatest hitters in baseball history.

30

fear the strain on his eyes would ruin him as a hitter.

Hornsby's hitting kept the struggling Cards going in the early 1920s as Rickey built his farm system and brought up younger players. It took time. The Cards struggled to sixth place in 1920 and finished third in 1921, fourth in 1922, fifth in 1923, and sixth in 1924. First baseman Jim Bottomley had a few good years, and hurler Jesse Haines won eighteen in 1921, but the cupboard was still nearly bare. Breadon, looking for a pennant, was depressed. So in the summer of 1925, as the Cards wallowed in last place, while Hornsby was hitting over .400, he made Hornsby manager. In 1926 the Cards got very lucky. They managed to land New York Giants outfielder Billy Southworth in a trade and then acquired Cubs pitcher Grover Cleveland ("Pete") Alexander, thirty-nine years old and fading fast, for just $4,000. Old Pete Alexander knew he had a few curves left in his tired arm. He proved it in his very first start, beating the team that had dumped him, the Cubs, 3–2, in ten innings in front of a roaring crowd of thirty-seven thousand, then the largest the Cards had ever seen. That win proved a turning point. Alexander won nine games for the Cards in two months, and Billy Southworth hit .317. Jim Bottomley, caught up in the fever, hit .299 with nineteen homers. Jesse Haines had a 13–4 record, and Flint Rhem won twenty games. Hornsby hit .317. Little by little, week by week, the Cards whittled away at the National League, and they clinched first place at

Grover Cleveland
Alexander, who
fought lifelong
battles against
epilepsy and alco-
holism, spent only
four years with the
Cardinals, but they
were among the
most memorable
seasons in the
team's history.

the tail end of a twenty-five game, end-of-the-season road trip forced by messy scheduling. All of Saint Louis celebrated the team's first pennant since the heyday of Van Der Ahe's teams of the 1880s. There were torch-light parades, rallies, speeches, and all-night celebrations. The Cardinals went into the World Series against Babe Ruth, Lou Gehrig, and the rest of the powerhouse New York

Yankees. Maybe it was the fact that they were long shots that pumped them up, or maybe it was just fate, but the Cards bounced back after losing the first game to beat the Yanks, 6–2 on the four-hit pitching of grizzled Pete Alexander and an inside-the-park homer by Tommy Thevenow.

Delighted with the split, the Cards returned to Saint Louis and beat the Yanks

Fans pile into Sportsman's Park to watch the Cardinals take on the Chicago Cubs during the championship 1926 season.

32

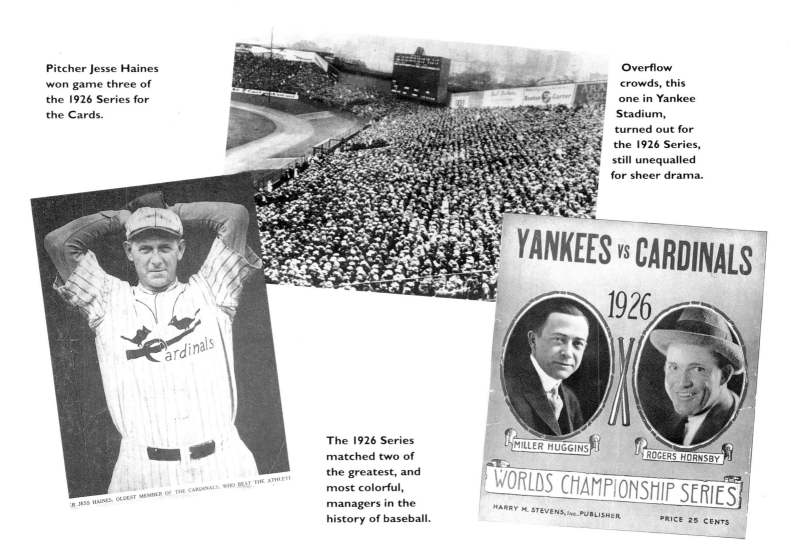

Pitcher Jesse Haines won game three of the 1926 Series for the Cards.

ER JESS HAINES, OLDEST MEMBER OF THE CARDINALS, WHO BEAT THE ATHLETI

Overflow crowds, this one in Yankee Stadium, turned out for the 1926 Series, still unequalled for sheer drama.

The 1926 Series matched two of the greatest, and most colorful, managers in the history of baseball.

YANKEES vs CARDINALS
1926
MILLER HUGGINS   ROGERS HORNSBY
WORLDS CHAMPIONSHIP SERIES
HARRY M. STEVENS, Inc., PUBLISHER   PRICE 25 CENTS

again, 4–0. Pitcher Jesse Haines not only won the game on the mound but hit a two-run homer. Enough of this, decided Ruth, and he stunned St. Louis the next day, hitting three homers in a single game, a record that stands to this day. One of his titanic blasts went right out of the park

and broke a window at the Wells Chevrolet Company. The Yanks evened the Series in that game with a 10–5 win. They won again the next day, 3–2, on Tony Lazzeri's tenth-inning sacrifice fly. The Series moved back to New York, and the Cards clobbered the Yanks on their own field, 10–2,

By the end of the 1920s, the nucleus of a great team (soon to be known as the "Gashouse Gang") was in place and poised to do great things.

with Alexander winning again, setting up the dramatic finale.

Much has been written about that game—Hollywood even made a movie about it, *The Winning Team,* with Ronald Reagan playing Alexander. The Cards led 3–2 in the seventh, and Jesse Haines, his hands bleeding from hurling more than

a hundred knuckleballs, was tiring fast. He had just loaded the bases, and Tony Lazzeri was up for the Yanks. Two outs, sixty-seven thousand people on their feet. Hornsby, against all the rules in the book, called in old Pete Alexander, tired from pitching a complete game the day before and, rumor had it, a long night on the

This annual team photo became a much-coveted collector's item after the October victory . . .

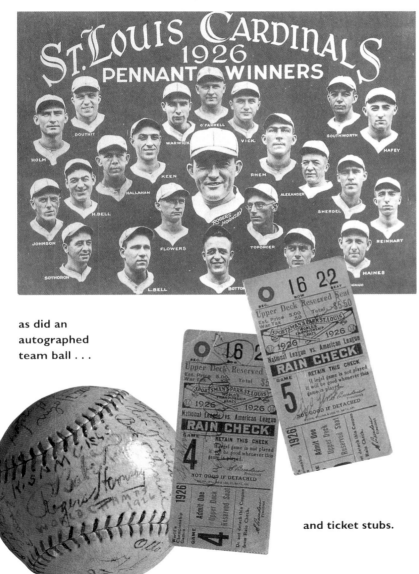

as did an autographed team ball . . .

and ticket stubs.

town. He looked awful. There was quiet throughout Yankee Stadium as Hornsby gave Alexander the ball. Hornsby reminded Alexander that there were two outs and the bases were loaded.

"Well," Alexander said slowly, rubbing the ball in his large hands, staring at the three men on the bases. "There's no place to put Tony, so I guess I'll have to strike him out."

Alexander worked Lazzeri to a one-and-one count, then watched in agony when the slugger ripped what appeared to be a long home run down the left-field line as the crowd thundered. It went foul by a foot, though, and Lazzeri went back to the batter's box. Alexander threw him a fastball and then, to fool him, a low, outside curve—"Strike three!" Alexander saved the inning. He came back in the eighth and ninth and put the Yanks down, winning the world championship.

Saint Louis went wild with glee, treating their conquering heroes to a succession of parties and parades. That world championship was the start of a long period of National League domination for the Cards, a stretch of eighteen years in which the Cards would win seven pennants and eight world championships. The fans went wild with anger just a few months after the 1926 victory, though, when the front office traded away their

Frank Frisch came to
Saint Louis in 1927,
and soon became a
fan favorite as he
played and managed
his way to one of the
most distinguished
careers in baseball.

manager, the greatest pure hitter in
baseball, Rogers Hornsby. Sam Breadon
and Branch Rickey couldn't stand Hornsby
anymore. During the fall they had a
number of disagreements with him and,
three .400 seasons or not, world title
or not, they decided he had to go. They
hadn't considered the chunk of stock
Hornsby owned in the club, though.
Hornsby wouldn't agree to a trade to
the Giants unless the Cards bought him
out—at inflated prices. The Cards
couldn't afford it and had to borrow

money from other National League owners to get rid of Hornsby.

The 1927 season started badly,
second-baseman Frankie Frisch, the
"Fordham Flash," was brought to St. Louis
from the New York Giants to replace
Hornsby, and fans booed him for the
first few weeks. Frisch was a fine player,
though, and finally won fans over with his
.337 average. The Cards finished second,
just one and a half games behind Pittsburgh. Not only did they miss out on the
pennant, but in late September a hurricane

nearly destroyed Sportsman's Park. Their fortunes were better in 1928, as the talented products of Rickey's farm system were beginning to excel on the parent club. Jim Bottomley, who hit .325, won the MVP award, and led the Cards to first place, two games ahead of the Giants. Frankie Frisch hit .300, George Harper .305, and Chick Hafey hit .337. A trade put the zany Rabbit Maranville at shortstop. On the mound, Jesse Haines and Bill Sherdel won more than twenty games each and Pete Alexander, now forty, won sixteen.

The 1928 Cardinals were better than the 1926 team but they were swept by the revenge-seeking Yankees, four games to none, in the World Series. Babe Ruth hit .625, with three home runs, and Lou Gehrig hit .545 with four homers. The Cards finished fourth in 1929. Pete Alexander retired that season, and manager Bill McKechnie was fired and replaced by Billy Southworth. The nucleus of a great team was there, though, and the farm stars were arriving regularly. The Cardinals were poised to do spectacular things in the 1930s.

Player cards were popular items in the victorious 1920s.

The 1926 Cardinals— that's old Grover Cleveland Alexander, at far right in the front row, will always be remembered as one of the finest teams baseball has ever seen.

CHAPTER THREE

THE GASHOUSE GANG

1930–1939

The yellow taxi sped through the streets of Manhattan, its wheels squealing as it turned corners and darted among cars, trucks, and pedestrians. The cab stopped with a jolt in front of the radio studio and its six passengers, jammed in like tabloid newspapers tied up in a bundle, tumbled out. Clothing rumpled, hair still wet from quick showers, the men, carrying musical instruments, ran across the sidewalk, spun through a revolving door, and rushed into an elevator. A few flights up they burst out of the elevator and, with just thirty seconds to air time, got ready to perform on Bob Ripley's "Believe It or Not" radio show, just as so many of the country's finest orchestras did.

This was the Mudcat Band, the extremely ad hoc orchestra of the St. Louis Cardinals baseball team. That particular night, the boys almost missed air time because their fiddler, pitcher "Fiddler Bill" McGee, had just tossed a one-hitter (and driven in the winning run himself) against the Brooklyn Dodgers. They certainly weren't the best band in the land, but they may have been the most entertaining. Left fielder Pepper Martin was master of ceremonies and played harmonica and guitar. Pitcher Lon Warneke, the "Arkansas Hummingbird," played guitar and sang. Pitcher Max Lanier spelled him as a crooner, and pitcher Bob Weiland blew tunes into a jug. Outfielder Frenchy Bordagaray played a gadget that was comprised of

Several members of the famous Gashouse Gang pose before they played in the 1935 All-Star game: from left to right, Burgess Whitehead, manager Frankie Frisch, Pepper Martin, Rip Collins, Joe Medwick, and Dizzy Dean.

Every kid in Saint Louis had a Card's Knot Hole Gang pass. You went to the ball game free any day but Sunday and you sat in left field. All you needed was a nickel for your snow cone, a nickel for the street car, and you were all set. I must have seen a thousand games in the 1930s with my Knot Hole Gang pass. Every kid in the neighborhood did.

—ERV FISCHER, 69,
CARDINALS HALL OF FAME HISTORIAN

The Cards, like just about every other team, had a Knot Hole Gang that let kids attend games at a discount.

a whistle, washboard, auto horn, and electric light. They dressed in cowboy outfits, boots, and wide-brimmed, straw sombreros and specialized in hillbilly and cowboy music, recording memorable hits such as "Willie, My Toes Are Cold," "Birmingham Cool," and "They Buried My Sweetie Under an Old Pine Tree." Throughout the 1930s, the Mudcat Band was booked on hundreds of radio shows and at countless nightclubs as the Cardinals crisscrossed the United States playing its National

League schedule. Ads in local newspapers urged residents in towns across the country to come see the team play in the afternoon and the Mudcat Band play at night.

Only the 1930s St. Louis Cardinals could tour America with its very own hillbilly band. The tip off that the team of that decade was going to be one of the zaniest collection of ballplayers in the history of the game came when Gabby Street was named manager in 1930. Street had been a fine coach for the team in 1929 and a

The great Leo "The Lip" Durocher wore this jersey and used this glove when he played for the Cardinals in the 1930s.

after missing the first fourteen. The team of like-minded characters that Street would adeptly guide through the 1930s was one of the best baseball teams in major-league history, winning three pennants and two world championships. The team also served as the foundation for the fine Cardinal teams of the 1940s, which would add four more pennants and three world championships to the Cards' record book.

The team became known as the Gashouse Gang when multitalented and slightly off-center shortstop Leo Durocher was asked if the Cards were as good as American League teams. He replied, "They wouldn't let us in the other league. They would say we are a lot of gashouse ballplayers." Durocher, a handsome man about town and the most nattily dressed ballplayer in the National League, got his job when the other shortstop, Charley Gelbert, accidentally shot himself on a hunting trip and was laid up for two seasons. In the fall of 1934, as the Cards fought gallantly to win the pennant, Leo just couldn't wait to marry Grace Dozier and kept badgering player-manager Frankie Frisch to let them tie the knot. Frisch kept insisting that Leo and Grace wait until the season was over so Durocher could keep his mind on baseball. Leo, with no need to explain how beautiful Grace was, insisted

superb manager in the Cards minor-league system, but he had earned his fame when, in a 1908 publicity stunt, he stood at the base of the Washington Monument and caught a baseball dropped from the top,

41

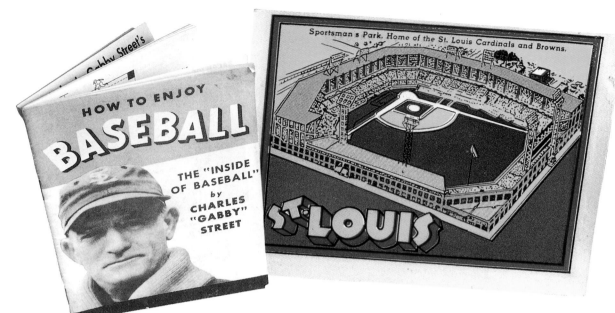

Gabby Street was named manager in 1930 and led the Cardinals to two pennants in Sportsman's Park.

that until he got married, he could only keep his mind on one thing—and it wasn't baseball. Finally, unable to wait a moment longer, Leo and Grace raced off to a local judge's office on the morning of September 25, in the middle of the last week of the tight pennant race, and got married. Just after saying "I do," Leo and best man Ernie Orsatti jumped in a cab and raced off to the ballpark, where the Cards beat the Giants, 3–2.

With their charm and their antics, as well as their talent, the Cardinals of the 1930s were one of the most beloved baseball squads of all time. Chunkily built outfielder Pepper Martin, the "Wild Horse of the Osage," became a crowd favorite with his head-first slides and clubhouse horseplay. He arrived at his first spring training in rumpled clothes and a two-day beard,

after spending the night in jail for hitchhiking. He once arrived at a hotel, shotgun slung under his arm, and registered as fabled gangster Pretty Boy Floyd. He was surrounded by unamused police in minutes. Ripper Collins played first base. For laughs, he and five teammates, including Dizzy Dean, once dressed up as carpenters, walked into the dining room of a Philadelphia hotel where a group of wealthy businessmen were attending a luncheon, began turning over tables, measuring the floors and walls, sawing wood, nailing planks to the walls, and shooing people out of the room. Outfielder Terry Moore became famous one day when, intent on scoring from first on a ball hit off the outfield wall, he paid no attention to the runner ahead of him on third. To avoid disaster, the third-base

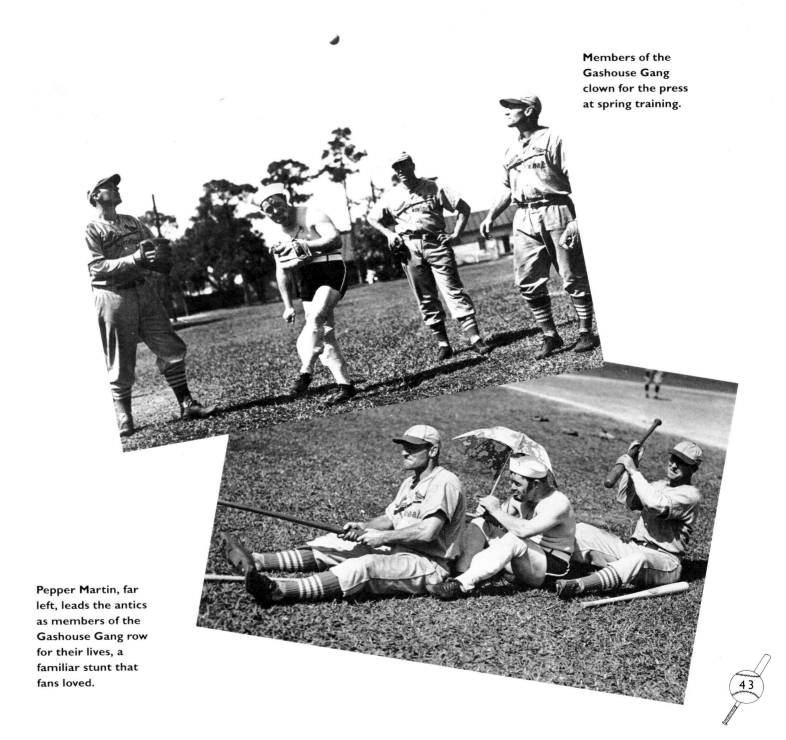

Members of the
Gashouse Gang
clown for the press
at spring training.

Pepper Martin, far
left, leads the antics
as members of the
Gashouse Gang row
for their lives, a
familiar stunt that
fans loved.

43

This 1931 souvenir hat is as outlandish as the antics of the Gashouse Gang. The 1936 Cardinals finished a respectable third.

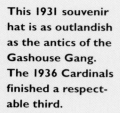

think as good as the players on the Gashouse Gang were said to be, they were still underrated. Tremendous ballplayers. They all hustled, every one of them. They'd be down nine to nothing in the ninth and play like crazy, convinced they could beat you. If Pepper Martin lost, he'd be furious with himself. Durocher would fume. They were all like that—loved to win and just hated to lose.

—BUDDY HASSETT, WHO PLAYED AGAINST THEM AS A BROOKLYN DODGER FROM 1938 TO 1940

The glove beneath the cards belonged to Jim Bottomley.

coach sent the runner on third home as Moore hurtled around third and right through the coach's hold-up sign. The runner on third slid into home plate and Moore slid right under his body, both pairs of feet crossing the plate at the same time and sending the umpire into total confusion. Both men were called safe.

In the off season Ernie "Showboat" Orsatti, an outfielder, was a professional boxer, football player, and auto racer, as well as a bit actor in Buster Keaton movies. Catcher Bill "Kayo" DeLancey was an eccentric of the first order and one of the chief pranksters on the team. After sitting out four seasons while battling tuberculosis, he made a remarkable comeback and returned to play fifteen games for the Cards in 1940. Harrison "Doc" Weaver, a chiropractor who was the team doctor, put hexes on opposing teams and players. Burleigh Grimes, a pitching ace obtained in a trade at the start of the 1930 season, had a skin disorder that caused blotches. To cover them, he always wore a two-day growth of beard, which made him look menacing. Wild Bill Hallahan, another pitcher, was either wildly good (he led the National League in strikeouts in 1930 and 1931) or wildly bad (he also led the National League in walks in 1930, 1931, and 1933). Dizzy Dean, the loquacious-philosopher king from Oklahoma, came up as a rookie in 1930 and soon joined in the Gang's high jinks. To stay warm during games in April, when it was still too cold for his tastes, he would gather some wood, start a bonfire in front of the Cardinal dugout in the first inning, and crouch next to it, rubbing his hands together.

Rookie manager Gabby Street did not have a championship club at the start of the 1930 season, but he did when it finished. Branch Rickey adroitly obtained Burleigh Grimes from Boston and got thirteen wins out of him in half a season. Rookie outfielder George Watkins came up from the farm system and hit .370. Every starter

The Cards made the headlines, and it was easy to forget that they shared Sportsman's Park with the Browns, two of whom are depicted on this 1935 baseball card.

46

The Browns pose for their 1935 team shot.

on the team, after slow beginnings, wound up hitting over .300. The Redbirds showed they were tough, too. By the middle of August, the team was in fourth place, a good twelve games behind the league-leading and talent-soaked Cubs. Fans winced when the Dodgers came to town on August 8 and pummeled the Cards, 11–5. However, instead of demoralizing the Cards, that pounding seemed to inspire them. They behaved like the skinny little kid pushed around by the school bully once too often. The Cardinals, every one of them, turned on the Dodgers and the whole National League. They whipped the Dodgers four straight. Then, pumped

up, they took three out of five from the Braves and were on their way. In the last six weeks of the season, the Cards went on a 21–3 streak to catch the Cubs and Dodgers and take the flag.

During the torrid stretch run, which brought in overflow crowds at just about every ballpark where the Cards played, the members of the Gashouse Gang were, of course, in the news all the time for their usual high jinks. In New York on the night of September 15, just before a big game with the Brooklyn Dodgers and the same night the Cubs and Giants faced off in the first game of a three-game series at the Polo Grounds, all three teams were

47

Paul Dean won the trophy in the foreground, and his teammates collected many others during the 1930s.

within one game of each other. Cards hurler Flint Rhem simply disappeared. Vanished. Nobody could find him. The next morning he showed up at Ebbets Field, and he was a mess. His clothes were dirty and rumpled, his hair uncombed, words slurred, and physical condition dreadful. He told Gabby Street he had been kidnapped. He was walking into the lobby of his hotel, he claimed, when two men grabbed him, forced him into a cab, and drove him to New Jersey. There, locked in a house, the men, gamblers who had bet thousands of dollars on the next day's game, forced him to drink liquor all night so he could not pitch the next day and beat their Dodgers. The story was so rich in detail and anecdote that Street actually believed him. He told Rhem to take it easy and recover. No problem, really, because he could start Wild Bill Hallahan instead. A few minutes later, Wild Bill jumped out of a taxi and slammed the door behind him—right on his finger. An enraged Street told Wild Bill he had to pitch anyway. Wild Bill did, holding the baseball right on top of his swollen finger, and the Cards won.

On the last day of the season, the pennant clinched, Street put a rookie just up from the minors on the mound to pitch. He threw a three-hitter. Later, Street said of him prophetically, "I think he is going to be a great one, but I'm afraid we'll never know from one minute to the next what he's going to do or say." The kid's name was Dizzy Dean.

The 1930 World Series was going to be a tough one. The Cards had to face the Philadelphia A's, who had won the 1929 World Series and were even stronger in 1930. The A's took game one, 5–2, and game two, 6–1. Back in Saint Louis, the

Cards managed to win games three and four behind the pitching of Wild Bill Hallahan and Jesse Haines. Game five went to the A's when Jimmie Foxx hit a two-run homer. Momentum on their side, the A's locked up their second straight title with an easy 7–1 victory in game six back in Philadelphia.

The Cards, beaten but not defeated, put together one of the finest teams in

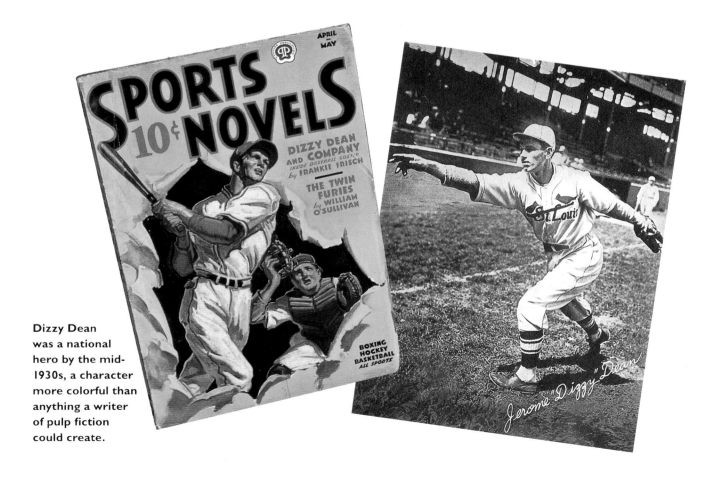

Dizzy Dean was a national hero by the mid-1930s, a character more colorful than anything a writer of pulp fiction could create.

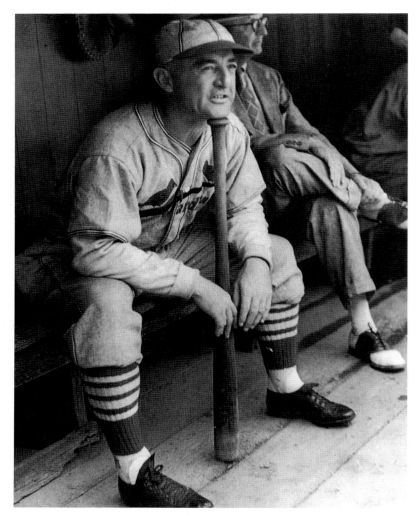

As player-manager, Frankie Frisch brought home a world championship for the Cards in 1934.

history in 1931 and won another pennant. Pepper Martin, one of the most popular players in Saint Louis history, arrived that year and hit .300, which on that team didn't mean much. He was just the sixth-best hitter. Chick Hafey hit a league-leading .349 and was followed by Jim Bottomley, with .348. Frankie Frisch hit .311. Taylor Douthit, another farm-system graduate, hit .331, and Ripper Collins hit .301. The pitching staff was solid, with Wild Bill Hallahan posting a 19–9 record following his 15–5 mark in 1930. Burleigh Grimes finished at 17–9, and new acquisition Paul Derringer went 18–8. The Cards won 101 games and took the flag at a gallop, thirteen games ahead of the Giants.

As always, they had trouble with the A's, who were looking for a third-straight world championship. Pepper Martin was the hero of the 1931 Series, putting on one of the great October performances of all time. He collected twelve hits, including a homer and four doubles, batted .500, stole five bases, drove in five runs, and scored five times. The A's were hard to put away, though. The Cards and the A's split the first four games. Then Martin hit a home run and four RBIs in game five to lead the Redbirds to a 5–1 win. But the A's bounced right back to take game six, 8–1. The Cards, denied the title in 1928 and 1930, fought back to win the seventh game 4–2 on a home run by young George Watkins, up from the farm system, and the last fly ball out was made by none other than Pepper Martin.

The Cards, a little bloated from celebrations that continued through the winter, tumbled all the way to seventh in 1932. Only George Watkins and Ernie Orsatti hit over .300. There was one wonderful omen, though. The talkative and charm-ing pitcher from Oklahoma, young Dizzy Dean, came into his own and won eighteen games. In 1933 the team started off badly, wallowing in last place for weeks. Gabby Street was fired. Pitcher Paul Derringer was traded, and Leo Durocher was brought in at shortstop. The Cards finished fifth, nine and a half games out of first, but placed four men on the All-Star team (Frankie Frisch, Pepper Martin, Jimmy Wilson, and Wild Bill Hallahan). Dizzy Dean got better, winning twenty games. Tex Carleton won seventeen, and Wild Bill Hallahan another sixteen.

Despite the fifth-place finish in 1933, the Cards were the darlings of Saint Louis going into the 1934 season. They had won four pennants in six years, looked promising for the next season, and had showcased some of the best pitchers and hitters in baseball. Attendance had climbed from 173,000 in 1919 to 623,000 in 1931. The Cards had their own loyalists, but they had also benefitted from the failures of their co-tenants at Sportsman's Park, the woeful St. Louis Browns. If baseball fans were going to choose between a pennant winner and a last-place team, it was going to be the pennant winner. Ironically, in the 1920s the Browns had expanded Sportsman's Park from eighteen-thousand to thirty-thousand seats, expecting better times. It was the Cards, not the Browns,

Leo Durocher was inducted into the Hall of Fame in 1994, and the recognition was long overdue. He was a fine infielder for the Cards before going on to greater fame as manager of the Dodgers, Giants, and Cubs.

DIZZY DEAN

Yes, it can indeed
be said . . . no one
will ever fill Dizzy
Dean's boots.

ike Theodore Roosevelt in politics and Groucho
Marx in film, Dizzy Dean was an original crea-
tion who transcended his sphere, baseball, and
became an American folk hero. He arrived in Saint
Louis and threw a three-hitter in his very first game
as casually as if he were going down to the corner
store to get a loaf of bread. He was a country boy, the
son of an Oklahoma sharecropper, and did not wear
shoes every day until he was in the army. He had rube
habits, shabby clothing, and a thick Oklahoma drawl
when he invaded the big city, and like the heros of
the Frank Capra movies, he remained just the way
he was and was idolized for it. He was his own inven-
tion, a real-life flesh-and-blood character bigger and
bawdier than a 1930s pulp-fiction writer could invent.

He was the greatest pitcher of his time—there's
no doubt about that. He won a game at age twelve
against a local college team, won more than twenty
games four major-league seasons in a row before
breaking his foot and sending his career into oblivion
in 1937. He won eighteen games and led the National
League in strikeouts his rookie year, just after turning twenty-one. During his remarkable 1932 to 1936
streak he averaged twenty-five wins and pitched 300
innings a year. A fine hitter, he batted .246 in 1934,
the year he won thirty games and the MVP Award,
and the Cards won the World Series.

But it was his antics and vibrant personality that
people enjoyed. Dean genuinely loved people, par-

ticularly kids, but he liked to taunt opponents. He once visited the Dodger clubhouse and told the players exactly how he would pitch to them that day—and then went out and threw a shut-out. He dropped in for a visit to the Giants dugout before a game and told manager Casey Stengel how he could win a pennant: "What you oughta do, Casey, is get yourself a pitcher like me and build a team around him. I'd hate to try and beat somebody like me."

Today's pitchers, after a win, will give reporters the usual patter about how tough it was to beat the other team and how much they owed their teammates. Not Dizzy. Dean said this after his win over Brooklyn one afternoon in 1934: "Boy, did I put it over on the Dodgers today." When he was asked how difficult it would be to beat the American League All-Stars in 1934, he shrugged and said, "Them guys? I could go on bread and water all week and beat them."

He didn't see it as boasting. "If you say you're gonna do somethin' and you do it, then it ain't braggin'," he said.

Unable to restrain his imagination, one day he told three different reporters that he was born in three different towns in three different states in three different years. Born Jay Hanna Dean, one day, in front of twenty reporters who needed copy, he simply invented a new name for himself—Jerome Herman Dean—and concocted a story about it being the

The Deans pitched for Union Leader as hard as they pitched for the Cards.

The famous hurler brothers signed this souvenir ball.

DIZZY DEAN

name of a dying boy who had asked Dizzy to use it to ease his father's grief.

He loved pranks, starting bonfires in front of dugouts to keep his hands warm on cold days, running down to the pit in theaters and conducting the orchestra to the delight of the crowd, jumping into the middle of a professional wrestling match to take on the villain. The tall, thin hurler, despite all his shenanigans, has a serious side, too. A major force in the integration of baseball, he barnstormed the country with black all-star teams, packing in crowds in city after city. It was the first time a white super-star banged on the door of baseball integration, and it had enormous effect.

Dizzy was traded to the Cubs after he broke his foot and struggled through three poor seasons in Chicago. He pitched in the minors for a while then became a legendary broadcaster for the Browns and Cardinals, where he enthralled a whole new generation of fans with his stories and malapropisms.

He once said of a man in the batter's box: "He's standing confidentially at the plate."

After a fly ball was caught: "The runners have returned to their respectable bases."

After a head injury: "The doctors X-rayed my head and found nothing."

Of the schedule: "Don't fail to miss tomorrow's game."

Baseball never saw his likes again.

Dizzy Dean's brother Paul, also a pitcher, joined the Cards in 1934, and was soon impressing fans himself.

during the 1933 season, looked around and saw a tremendous team: first base, Ripper Collins (.333 and thirty-five homers); second base, Frisch himself (.305); shortstop, Leo Durocher (.260); third base, Pepper Martin (.289); right field, Ernie Orsatti (.300); left field, Ducky Medwick (.319); center, Spud Davis (.300); catcher, Kayo DeLancey (.316). On the mound Frisch had Tex Carleton (16–11), and Bob Walker (12–4). And in the warm spring of 1934 Dizzy Dean talked Branch Rickey into hiring his brother Paul (immediately nicknamed Daffy), also a pitcher who was then playing in the Texas League.

"Hell," Dizzy bragged to reporters, "me and Paul will win forty-five games this year." That was Dizzy's year, just as 1927 was Babe Ruth's year and 1941 was Joe DiMaggio's year. The Deans did not win forty-five games—they won forty-nine. Daffy took nineteen games and Dizzy had one of the greatest years of any pitcher in any league, winning thirty. Everything went right for Dizzy and Daffy that year, and the effervescent Dizzy had a great line for the sportswriters when things went right. During a September 21 doubleheader, Dizzy threw a three-hitter to take game one, 13–0, then Daffy threw a no-hitter to win game two, 3–0. In the clubhouse, Dizzy, his smile wide, told the reporters, "I wish that kid had told me he was going

who sold all those extra seats. The Browns were so bad that in 1936 they averaged only twelve hundred people per game.

When spring training began for the 1934 season, player-manager Frankie Frisch, who had taken the helm from Gabby Street

Dizzy and Daffy liked to clown for photographers, but on the field they were all business.

to pitch a no-hitter. If I knew that, I'd have thrown one, too."

The Deans were so hot in the final week of the season that they pitched five of the last six games, winning every one. Dizzy took the last game of the season, his thirtieth win, with a 9–0 shutout to clinch the pennant. The national press loved to cover the Dean brothers as they rambled from city to city, signing autographs in hotel lobbies, appearing in cigarette ads, leading orchestras at night clubs for fun, showing up at schools to meet kids, and

charming crowds with their Oklahoma drawls. Sportswriter Grantland Rice commented in the *New York Sun,* "As the bulky figure of Babe Ruth fades out of the picture, an old-fashioned schooner fading into the fog, two kids from the dust of the Western trail take his place as the greatest sensations baseball has known—matching the glamour of Mathewson, Hans Wagner, Ty Cobb and Babe Ruth. . . ."

The Deans did not cool off a bit in October when they went up against the American League champion Detroit Tigers

The crusader gracing this program went home happy—the Cardinals won the 1934 World Series, four games to three. Paul Dean hurled the ball, center, in his 1934 no-hitter against Brooklyn. Even when Babe Ruth wasn't playing in a Series, he still managed to make an appearance; here he greets managers and players before the 1934 classic.

in the World Series. They each won two games, and the Cards took the series in seven games, aided by Pepper Martin's eleven hits and Leo Durocher's sensational fielding. "Leo the Lip," hitless until game six, lashed three hits, including the hit that brought in the winning run in the sixth game, to send the series to a climactic game seven. Dizzy was in perfect form that final game in Detroit and threw a six-hit shutout against the Tigers, as his mates hammered out seventeen hits in an 11–0 victory. (Dizzy got two hits himself.)

The victory was marred, though, by an ugly episode involving Ducky Medwick. In the third inning, Medwick slid into third

baseman Marv Owen, spikes up, and hurt him. Heated words were exchanged. The Detroit crowd became surly, and in the fourth, when Medwick trotted out to play left field, fans started to boo. By the fifth they were pelting Medwick with programs. In the sixth, as the Cards were running up the score, fans turned ugly and started pelting Medwick with vegetables, fruit, scorecards, and soda bottles. Workers had to be sent to left field each inning to clear the debris. The umpires and Tigers players pleaded with the fans to stop the barrage, to no avail. So much junk was hurled into left field at the start of the seventh inning that commissioner Kenesaw Landis, fearful

A pin from the 1930s.

Detroit fans pelted Ducky Medwick, number seven, with debris after he slid hard into third in game seven of the 1934 Series.

of a full-scale riot, ordered Medwick out of the game, the only time a player has ever been pulled out of a game by a commissioner. The brutality of the crowd inspired veteran sportswriter Paul Gallico to write in the *New York Daily News,* "It was a terrifying sight. Every face in the crowd, women and men, was distorted with rage. Mouths were torn wide, open eyes glistened and shone in the sun. All fists were clenched."

The Cardinals were just as good in 1935. Medwick hit .353, Collins hit .313, and Spud Davis hit .317. Dizzy Dean had a 28–12 record, and Daffy finished 19–12. The Cards were sitting comfortably in first

on Labor Day. Fate intervened, however, as the Chicago Cubs, eager for their first flag since 1932, won twenty-one straight games and took the pennant.

In 1936, the Cards had another great team, despite catastrophic health problems. Daffy Dean's arm went dead, and he won just five games. Kayo DeLancey contracted tuberculosis. Frankie Frisch hurt his foot and missed more than sixty games. But there were bright spots. Dizzy Dean, unquestionably the best pitcher in baseball by the summer of 1936, won twenty-four games, the fourth year in a row he had taken twenty or more wins. Rookie Johnny Mize was brought up from the minors and hit .329. It wasn't enough, though, and the Cards finished five games in back of the Giants.

The year 1937 belonged to Ducky Medwick. He hit .374 with 237 hits and 154 RBIs to win the batting title and the MVP award. Mize, in his first full year in the majors, became a superstar by hitting .364 with twenty-five homers. The year certainly didn't belong to the Dean Brothers. Daffy, his arm gone, was out of the majors, playing in the minors as part of a rehabilitation program that would fail miserably. Dizzy started off the year by taking a swing at a New York sportswriter during spring training, instigated an on-field melee in midseason, and got into a bitter feud

This luxurious sweater, in Cardinal red, belonged to Dizzy Dean.

Dizzy Dean, center, clowns before a 1933 game.

with league commissioner Ford Frick over the balk rule. Then, in a stroke of horrendous luck, during the 1937 All-Star game a sharp line-drive by Earl Averill hit Dizzy in the right foot, breaking it. That accident ruined him. He never pitched the same way again, and finished the year 13–10. Dean always claimed the club made him start playing again before his foot had mended. The club claimed the injury wrecked his delivery and weakened him. At the end of the season, knowing the sensational pitcher was finished at just

twenty-seven years old, Rickey sold Dizzy to Chicago, where after three seasons he had struggled back to sixteen wins. That winter Leo Durocher was traded to Brooklyn, and Frankie Frisch was fired. The Cards slumped to a sixth-place finish in 1938. By the beginning of the 1939 season, Wild Bill Hallahan and Rip Collins had been traded. Ernie Orsatti, Jesse Haines, and Kayo Delancey had retired. Ducky Medwick and Pepper Martin would be traded in 1940. The Gashouse Gang was running out of gas.

THE MEN AND THE MAN
1940–1949

The twenty-three thousand Cardinals-lovers fidgeted in their seats in both decks of old, open-sided Sportsman's Park. It was the warm night of June 4, 1940, and the first at-home night game of the year. What was unfolding on the field was, to fans used to the success of the Gashouse Gang, a nine-act tragedy. The Cards came into the game drifting in sixth place. They had almost won the pennant the year before, finishing four games out, and everyone thought they'd hoist one up the flagpole in 1940. Inning by inning, the visiting Dodgers thrashed the Redbirds on the field. The Cards' pitching was dreadful. Manager Ray Blades, in his second year, again used up four pitchers in another losing effort. The hitting was gone, and the weather was muggy and hot. The fans started to boo. A few innings later, thousands of them stood and held their noses to show their unhappiness with the team. Then they started to throw things. At first, they threw balls of paper, which came down like a snow shower from the upper deck. Then the fans chucked programs, pencils, and even soda bottles on to the field. Ice creams landed with a splat on the grass. High above, Sam Breadon, jacket off, tie unraveled, his shirt sticking to his skin from the heat, had enough. He needed new leadership—fast.

The new manager was Billy Southworth, a man who had learned

The 1944 World Series was one of three the Cardinals won during the decade. They played all seven games of this one in Sportsman's Park, against the other hometown team, the Browns.

61

Frederick Lieb's history of the Cardinals was published in the 1940s, an era when small pennants were all the rage among fans.

many lessons over the years and was getting not a second, but a third, chance in life. Southworth, who played with the pennant-winning Cardinals in the 1920s, did a brief stint as the team's manager in 1929 but was fired because he was too forceful with the players. Wanting to give Billy the Kid a second chance, Branch Rickey made him manager of the system's Rochester, New York, minor-league club in the late summer of 1929. Southworth won three straight pennants but never really got along with players there, either, and, becoming increasingly bitter that the Cards had let

him go, quit the organization in 1933 to coach the Giants. Rickey talked him into returning to manage Rochester in 1935. There, Southworth, learning from his mistakes, toned down his style and started to win again.

Billy wasn't going to blow his chance to coach the Cards this time. When he joined the team the second week in July 1940 he found a talented group of players who were not working together. The new Billy held the reins on the players loosely and even let the team stop off for a night in New York on their way to Boston to

Stan Musial went into full swing in the 1940s and didn't slow down a bit over the next two decades.

Slaughter hit .306, and Johnny Mize crushed forty-three homers.

In 1941, the last sweet summer before the United States entered World War II, the Cards were the team to beat, but, unfortunately, an unprecedented string of injuries all but crippled the team. Johnny Mize broke his finger. Infielder Jimmy Brown broke his right hand sliding into third base. Second baseman Frank Crespi was out for a month with an injury. Catcher Walker Cooper broke his collar bone and shoulder blade. Pitcher Mort Cooper was out for seven weeks following elbow surgery. On August 10 Enos Slaughter and Terry Moore collided chasing a fly ball, and Slaughter broke his collar bone. Two weeks later, Moore was hit in the head by a pitch and hospitalized. Despite everything, Southworth got his team through the year in second place, just two games out of first.

Needing a replacement for outfielder Slaughter, Rickey decided to take a chance on a ballplayer named Stan Musial. The kid rose up through the minor leagues as a terrific pitcher but fell on his arm and ruined it. He became an outfielder and quickly began to be noticed. Playing for Springfield, Massachusetts, in just eighty-seven games he hit .369, with twenty-six home runs. A year later, in fifty-seven games in Rochester, New York, he hit

see a championship fight. In return, the Cardinals played for Billy. They played hard and moved slowly up the ladder in the late summer of 1940 to finish a very respectable third, winning sixty-three of the games they played under Billy in 1940. Enos

Catcher Walker Cooper, left, and brother Morton, a pitcher, comprised one of the most successful combinations in baseball history.

over, number six. He put it on. The rest is not just history, it is lore.

Stan the Man sizzled right from the start with that peculiar toes-turned-in stance of his, hitting .426 in the last twelve games of the 1941 season. He would go on to hit .331 lifetime, with 475 home runs and 1,951 RBIs. He would be named MVP three times, lead the league in batting seven times, and be named to twenty All-Star teams in his twenty-two years as a Cardinal. He hit .310 or better in sixteen of his seasons—and Musial did it all with a pleasant, even-tempered demeanor, got along with everyone, and managed not only to be lionized in Saint Louis but in every National League city where he played.

In 1942, the Man hit .315 (and Enos Slaughter out-hit him at .318). Musial's obvious promise helped fans forget the ridiculous trade of Johnny Mize to the Giants, where he would continue his march into the Hall of Fame (that trade had been Rickey's biggest blunder). Other fine players on the 1942 team were Jimmy Brown (third base), Slats Marlon (shortstop), and Johnny Hopp (first base). Pitcher Mort Cooper, his arm healed, won twenty-two games, and young starter Johnny Beazley won twenty-one. The Cardinals had to outplay the streaking Dodgers, who were even better in 1942, winning 104 games, than they had been in 1941, when they beat the

.327. Rickey, pleased at the unusual turn of events for his hurler turned slugger, brought Musial up to the Cards on September 17, 1941. Musial had an unusually large torso and most uniform jerseys didn't fit him. There was only one that did, a left-

Cardinals out of the pennant. In August and September, the Redbirds played superior baseball, beating the Dodgers in a key series to take the flag by a thin, two-game margin, ending the season with 106 wins.

Exhausted by the tight pennant race, the Cards then had to face the fierce New York Yankees in the World Series, the awesome team that had won eight world championships in the past fifteen years, posting a formidable 32–4 record in them. The Cards were good with 106 wins, but the Yankees had won almost as many, 104. The Cards had Musial and Slaughter, but the Yanks had Joe DiMaggio (.305, twenty-one home runs), Charlie Keller (.292,

twenty-six home runs), Joe Gordon (.322), Bill Dickey (.295), and Phil Rizzuto (.284).

The Bronx Bombers started off just as the sportswriters predicted, with pitcher Red Ruffing going into the eighth inning with a no-hitter and a 7–0 lead. He gave up two hits in the eighth and gave up four runs to Saint Louis in the ninth. Even though the Yankees won, it was an omen. The Cardinals were ahead 3–0 in the eighth inning of game two when the Yankees' Charlie (King Kong) Keller crushed a three-run homer to tie the game. But the Cards bounced back quickly. Musial drove in Slaughter to give the Cards a 4–3 lead. Then, in the bottom

The Cards got good press in the 1940s: a 1943 Series press pass; a 1944 press pin; and a 1942 press pin.

65

Champs they were in 1943, but the Cards lost the Series that year to the Yankees.

Fans were ebullient in 1942 and 1943, but no one could forget we were at war.

of the ninth, with a mighty heave Slaughter threw out Tuck Stainback at third to preserve the win.

More than sixty-nine thousand fans jammed Yankee Stadium for game three to see pitcher Ernie White, just 7–5 for the year, shut out the Bronx Bombers, 2–0, the first time the Yankees had been shut out in a World Series game in sixteen years. The next day, the Cards beat the Yanks 9–6. The Cards wrapped it up in game four, 4–2, on a home run by third

baseman Whitey Kurowski. Not only had the Cardinals beaten the invincible Yankees, but they had thrashed them four straight and nailed the coffin shut in Yankee Stadium in front of almost seventy-thousand disbelievers.

Most of the players on the 1942 team, the youngest ever to win a National League pennant, had been nurtured in Rickey's vast farm system. They were brought up slowly, from A-level to AAA-level teams, and seasoned. When the call

Let's go see the Cardinals . . . and the Browns. The 1944 Cards were great, and they met the other home team in the Series.

came, they were ready. The 1942 team was a no-nonsense, just-business ball club. They would dominate the National League for the rest of the 1940s, finish first four times, second five times, and take three World Series. The 1942 Cardinals roster included a lot of young fathers who were exempt from the draft, but by the spring of 1943 the services had taken Terry Moore, Enos Slaughter, Johnny Beazley, Creepy Crespi (he broke his leg several times in the war and never played ball again), Jimmy Brown, Howie Pollet (he threw three consecutive shutouts before he went in), and Murry Dickson. Some players were exempt from military service because they were classified 4F or 1A due to injuries

or childhood diseases. Shortstop Marty Marion's was leg held together with wire from a childhood injury, but he could still play baseball (and he played pro football, too). Stan Musial was lost in the paperwork at his draft board. Perfectly able and perfectly willing to go in the spring of 1942, he was not called up until 1944. Rickey, who was in the war himself within the year, reached down into the farm system to bring up outfielder Harry Walker and second baseman Lou Klein, and pitchers Harry Brecheen, George Munger, and Alpha Brazle.

Musial had a tremendous year in 1943, hitting .357. Marion hit .280, and catcher Walker Cooper, Mort's brother,

STAN MUSIAL

I saw Stan Musial play the very first time I went to the ballpark. He was a great ballplayer, but to me he symbolized the small-town boy in the big city. He was certain of his skills but seemed a little out of place, in a very good way.
—GORDON DAVIS, 63, WENTZVILLE, MISSOURI

Dozens of commemorative buttons honor Musial's long career, but the statuette and autographed ball may be the best.

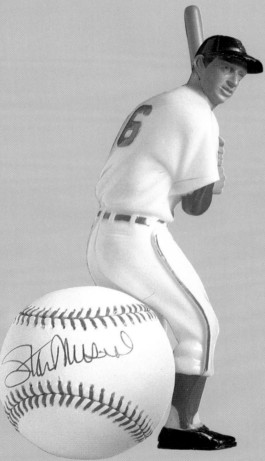

Stan Musial not only defined the ballplayer, he also defined the role of the ballplayer in his relation to the fans and to the game of baseball. Few other players have achieved the popularity Musial did, and only a few can match his statistics. He was a lifelong ambassador for the game of baseball and built bridges between players and fans that have lasted nearly sixty years.

Musial's numbers are awesome. He hit .331 lifetime over a career that saw him face just about every top pitcher in the National League. In addition to his consistent hitting, he was a feared power hitter who belted 475 homeruns and collected 1,951 RBIs.

Musial's uniform, bats, and trophies highlight a five-thousand piece Musial collection housed at the Cardinals Hall of Fame at Busch Stadium.

STAN MUSIAL

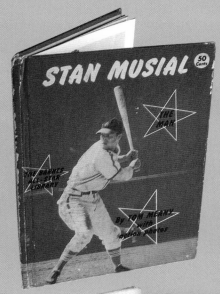

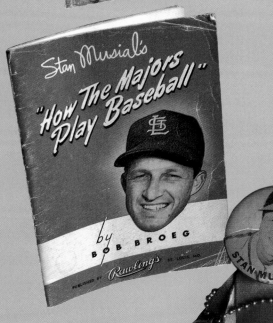

This special booklet commemorates one of the Cards greatest heroes ever, while in another booklet Musial shared his expertise with his public.

He won the Most Valuable Player Award three times (1943, 1946, and 1948) and led the league in hitting seven times. He made the All-Star team nineteen times.

And he never wanted to be a hitter. Musial joined the Cards' minor-league system as a pitcher and was soon posting an 18–5 record while hitting .356. A diving catch in the outfield in the summer of 1940 wrecked his left shoulder and ended his pitching career. His manager, Dickie Kerr, convinced him to turn himself into a fulltime hitter. The next season, Musial hit .426 and was brought up to the Cards.

Musial won his first league batting title in his second full season in the majors. He was not only a lethal hitter, for average or power, but was uncannily consistent. He averaged thirty-one home runs a season from 1948 to 1957, and from 1948 to 1954 he never hit less than .330. He averaged more than 100 RBIs a season from 1946 to 1957. Musial was a pitcher's nightmare. When asked how to pitch to him successfully, the Dodgers' Preacher Roe said, "Try to pick him off first base after he gets on."

It seems that just about everybody has a Stan Musial story to tell, whether it's the couple who got his autograph in a restaurant or the little boy who talked to him about baseball at the ballpark. His special relationship with kids was immortalized in Norman Rockwell's cover for the *Saturday Evening Post,* showing Musial signing autographs for children

These rings were presented to Musial over his long career, and Stan the Man's name emblazoned just about every object imaginable.

at the ballpark. He seemed to accept every invitation from every civic group in the state of Missouri.

There is a plaque for "Stan the Man" in the Hall of Fame and a lifesize statue of him in front of Busch Stadium, but he will live on not only in brass and bronze. He will live on in people's memories as one of the best—and nicest—players of all time.

Stan Musial was a truly wonderful man—no airs about him at all. Whether you were Harry Truman or the guy in the supermarket, he treated you the same. I wish the ballplayers today could have seen Stan Musial, to see how the superstars are supposed to act.

—PAUL LEPEER, 58, BLUFFTON, INDIANA

In 1944, the two home teams met on the same field for the Series. Saint Louis was ecstatic.

hit .318. Mort won twenty-one games. The Redbirds were strong and, following an eleven-game winning streak in July, raced on to win 105 games and take their second-straight pennant by a gap of eighteen games. Despite all that firepower, though, they lost the Series to the Yankees, four games to one.

In 1944, baseball generated as much excitement in Saint Louis as the World's Fair had in 1904. The Cardinals won their third straight pennant, again taking 105 games. Musial hit .347, but the MVP award

went to Marty Marion. He hit only .267, but was a brilliant fielder and earned the award for his glove. The really delightful surprise in Saint Louis that summer, though, was the startling success of the St. Louis Browns. The lowly Browns took the American League pennant, winning the last four games of the season and toppling the mighty, if war-diluted, Yankees. The success of both the Cardinals and the Browns set up the first and only all–Saint Louis World Series. It was also the first time the two tenants of one ballpark had

72

The Cards took the 1944 Series over the Browns, but it was a contest Saint Louis will never forget.

played each other since the Yankees and Giants shared the Polo Grounds when they met in the 1921 and 1922 Series.

Saint Louis was one huge blast of cacophonous noise that October. "You couldn't very well lose, could you?" remembers Louis Columbo, now eighty, who saw that series. "Both teams had hometown heroes. No matter who won, Saint Louis won. It was a time, all right. For a week before that Series everybody was arguing over who was going to win it. Most people favored the Cards, with the

power they had. But a lot of fans were kind of hoping the Browns would win just because they had been so bad for so long." Indeed, by the time the first game opened, the Browns, underdogs for forty years, suddenly found new legions of fans buying their programs and waving their pennants. It was a moment in the sun for the Browns, and they planned to make the most of it.

The Browns won the first game, 2–1, and they took the Cards to the eleventh inning of the second game before the

The Cards got a lot of press coverage in 1944, whatever the event, and adver- tisers didn't miss the chance to attach themselves to the champs.

One-month-old Johnny Hopp Jr., whose dad is one of the outfielders of the St. Louis Cardinals, protested in this way when his parents decided to have his first picture taken with his father's baseball hat, bat and a ball. The umpires finally reversed their decision.

Redbirds won, 3–2, on a single by pinch hitter Ken O'Dea. The Browns came back and won game three, 6–2, but lost game four when Musial hit a two-run homer. The Cards moved ahead in game five on a 2–0 shutout by Cooper, who fanned twelve, and they took the series in game six on a combined three-hitter pitched by Max Lanier and Ted Wilks. The second world championship in three years made Saint Louis the dominant team in the National League and was the last hurrah for the Browns, who would be gone from baseball in ten years.

The war was coming to an end in the spring of 1945, but there was a war brewing in the Cardinals' front office. Branch Rickey had gone over to the Brooklyn Dodgers when he returned from the war, and Sam Breadon, without Rickey to help him, was under fire from different enemies. He fought back. The Boston Braves had secretly approached Billy Southworth about leaving the Cards and becoming the Braves manager. Southworth told Breadon, who told him to go ahead and leave and hired Eddie Dyer as skipper. Breadon feuded with the Cooper brothers, and traded Mort to the Braves and sold Walker to the Giants.

In 1946, when everyone was back from the war, the Cards found themselves in a tight pennant race. Stan Musial, who won the MVP, hit .365, with 103 RBIs. Shortstop Marty Marion led the league in putouts and assists. Whitey Kurowski hit .301. Howie Pollet won twenty-one games, Harry Brecheen won fifteen, and Murry Dickson won fifteen. To make up for the stars they lost, the Cards turned to others. Rookie catcher Joe Garagiola hit only .247, but was superb defensively. Red Schoendienst, the young shortstop, seemed like the hero of a boys' adventure story. He and a friend hitchhiked to Saint Louis for one of the Cards' annual tryouts. With his

Stan the Man was one of several sports stars who pushed Wheaties in the 1940s.

bright red hair flying out from under his cap on steals, he was so impressive that the Cardinals signed him on the spot and sent him to a farm club the very next day. Red was unprepared for anything beyond the tryout, and the coaches had to give him lunch money. He moved up quickly. He hit .278 in 1945, his rookie year, .281 in 1946. He was also one of the top fielders in 1946, when he was moved from the outfield to second base.

Joe Garagiola never caught more than eighty-one games for the Cards, but the hometown player went on to glory as a broadcaster.

Enos Slaughter, who hit over .300 in the four years before his military service, hit a crisp .300 with a league-leading 130 RBIs. Slaughter, who had come up through the farm system, hit over .300 ten times and was a fine outfielder. He was unpopular with the large black population of Saint Louis, though, after he tried to organize players to strike when Jackie Robinson began playing major-league ball in 1947.

The Dodgers tied the Cardinals on the final day of the 1946 season, forcing a three-game playoff for the pennant. The Cards beat the Dodgers in the first two games to take the flag, then found themselves facing the Boston Red Sox in one of the most exciting World Series of all times. The American League champs had not won a Series since 1918 and were eager. The teams split the first two games, but the Red Sox surged ahead, taking game three by a score of 4–0. The see-saw went the other way the next day, when the Cards, unleashing twenty hits, thrashed the Sox, 12–4, knotting the Series at two games each. Then the Red Sox won game five. The Cards took game six, 4–1, setting up the dramatic finale. Enos Slaughter's miraculous dash in the eighth inning of the seventh game of the 1946 World Series was high Hollywood melodrama. He stroked a single in the bottom of the inning, with the game tied

Loved in St. Louis

ENOS SLAUGHTER . . .

up sentimental following i
Louis with his rugged p

to give full chances to three
outfielders—Wally

Enos Slaughter scored from first to win the 1946 World Series, a feat that made him a hero in Saint Louis.

3–3, and held first base as the next two batters went down. With two out and Harry Walker up, Slaughter took off for second. Walker connected and drove the ball into left-center field. Slaughter, nearly at second when Walker made the hit, made up his mind to go home. "It would be close, but I knew I could make it. I had

a good jump, the ball was hit deep. My chances were pretty good. I wanted to win the ball game," he remembers. "I never, never thought of holding up at third."

As every single person at Sportsman's Park rose, screaming, Enos headed for the plate. Boston shortstop Johnny Pesky held the ball a split second before he threw it

Slaughter races home all the way from first for the run that won the 1946 Series against Boston.

home. Amid the roar of the crowd and spray of the dirt, Slaughter slid in as the catcher's glove came down on him. *Safe.* The Cardinals, who held the Sox in the ninth, had won their third world championship of the decade.

The Cards finished second to the Dodgers in 1947. At the end of the season, Sam Breadon sold the team to businessman Robert Hannegan and died two years later. The 1948 Cards were again strong and again second. Stan Musial hit .376 with thirty-nine homers and 131 RBIs. He missed the Triple Crown by one homer, but won the MVP award— again. (When a reporter asked Carl Erskine of the Brooklyn Dodgers how he pitched to Musial, he said, "I just throw him my best stuff, then run over

By the time Sam Breadon stepped down, the Cards were the darlings of baseball, appearing on magazine covers and inspiring card games.

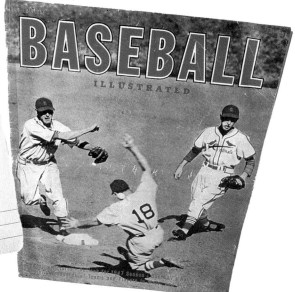

to back up third base.") Pitcher Murry Dickson was traded that year to Pittsburgh, for whom he won twenty games in 1951.

The forties ended in disappointment for Saint Louis. Again the best club in the league in 1949, they again rolled into first place and stayed there most of the summer, enjoying a two-and-a-half-game lead with ten to go. The fates, and the Dodgers, were not kind, however, and Brooklyn slowly edged ahead, taking the pennant by a single game on the very last day of the season. The Cardinals had reigned supreme in the 1940s, finishing in first or second in each season except 1940. But all that was about to change.

CHAPTER FIVE

DEATH AND REBIRTH
1950–1969

I n many ways, the 1950s were a good decade for the Cardinals. Brewery baron August Busch bought the team in 1953 (Sportsman's Park became Busch Stadium), providing financial stability and building even stronger ties between the Redbirds and the people of Saint Louis. Stan Musial established himself as one of the greatest ballplayers in history, leading the National League in batting four times (with a high of .351 in 1957) and making the All-Star team every single year he played. Musial not only set numerous baseball records, but in 1958 he became the first National Leaguer ever to break the six-figure mark, with his record $100,000.

But Busch and Musial could not make the Cardinals of the 1950s fly. At the end of the decade, critics had more theories to explain the decline than there were bottles of Budweiser beer in the state of Missouri. They said the death of Sam Breadon in 1949 undermined the team's longtime stability. They went back to 1943 and said Breadon should never have let Rickey go. They said Busch was a beer man, not a baseball man, that the stars of the 1940s should never have been traded, that Marty Marion should never have been hired as a manager. They said Busch and general manager Frank Lane should never have gone outside the Cardinal family to hire Eddie Stanky as manager. They said the team didn't bring young

Stan Musial's odd, pigeon-toed batting stance looked awkward, but it worked for him: He hit .331 during his twenty-two-year career.

81

**The 1950s saw ups
and downs for the
Cardinals. Score-
cards were colorful
and Stan Musial
modeled for a
Norman Rockwell
painting of the typi-
cal baseball player,
but the Saigh scandal
rocked baseball . . .**

players up fast enough, and that young players were brought up too soon. The critics
blamed Busch, Lane, the farm system, the
commissioner's office, the National League,
the American League, the press, and the
currents of the Mississippi River.

The catastrophic slide of the decade
started right away, in 1950, when the team
slipped to fifth place. Stan Musial led the
league in hitting again with a .346 mark,
but just about all the other aver-ages fell.
Marty Marion hit only .247, catcher Del
Rice .244 and Slaughter .290. Pitcher
Howie Pollet struggled to a 14–13 mark,
and Lanier pitched just 11–9. Manager

Eddie Dyer was gone at the end of the
season, replaced by Marty Marion, who
ran afoul of club owner Ed Saigh. He,
too, was soon gone, serving a prison
sentence for tax evasion. Then came
Eddie Stanky, brought in as fresh blood
from the Dodgers. Stanky was confron-
tational and feuded with just about
everybody. Busch, looking for a little stability, kept him on through mid-1955,
then let him go. The Cards were third
in 1952, when Schoendienst hit .303 and
Musial hit .336, fourth in 1953 (Schoendienst hit .342), sixth in 1954, and seventh
in 1955.

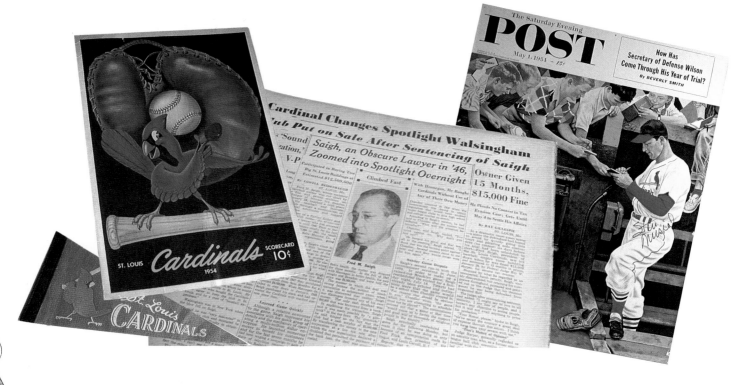

and the trade of Enos
Slaughter to the
Yankees irked fans.

Like most teams,
the Cards issued
photo sets in the
early 1950s.

Fans launched a storm of protests in 1954 when the front office suddenly traded Enos Slaughter to the Yankees. In 1956 Schoendienst was traded away. Bill Virdon, who would be a star for the Pirates, was obtained to replace Slaughter in 1954, but in 1956 he, too, was traded, to Pittsburgh. By 1957 just about every star of the recent past, except Stan Musial, was gone. Then

the papers leaked the unthinkable—general manager Frank Lane was actually talking of trading the beloved Stan the Man. As soon as Busch heard of it, he told Lane in no uncertain terms that Stan Musial was never, ever, to be traded.

The trades were a boon to the teams that got the former Cardinals players. Enos Slaughter hit .315 for the Yankees the year

The 1954 team looked great . . .

after he was traded and .304 in 1958, just before he retired. Schoendienst hit .302 for the Giants and for the Braves, and he hit over .300 in two seasons when he was brought back home to Saint Louis in 1960. Bill Virdon hit .334 in Pittsburgh the year he was traded. Most of the new players the Cards brought in to replace the trades were not much help at first. The Cards were fourth in 1956, fifth in 1958, and seventh in 1959. Manager Fred Hutchinson, on board for two years, got the Cards up to second in 1957, thanks to a good year

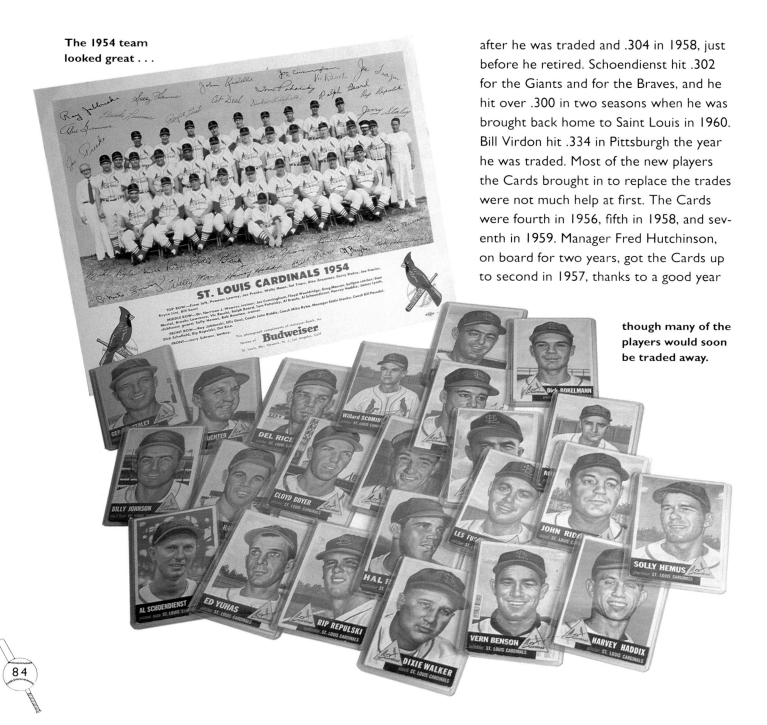

though many of the players would soon be traded away.

The Cards traveled to Japan, and welcomed the 1957 All-Star Game.

Wally Moon was the spirit of Saint Louis baseball in the mid-1950s.

from Stan Musial (.351, 29 home runs, 102 RBIs) and some fine pitching from Sam Jones, Lindy McDaniel, and Larry Jackson. Attendance, averaging about 1.2 million a year in the late 1940s, had slipped to about 900,000 a year in the 1950s.

Gloomy as the situation was as the decade drew to a close, several players were maturing, and others were arriving who would not only reverse the fortunes of the team, but bring the Cardinals back to the glory years of the 1940s.

Julian Javier played second base for the Cards for twelve years, earning recognition as one of the game's best fielders.

Stan Musial continued to grace baseball covers throughout the 1950s.

Under manager Solly Hemus, the Cards finished a respectable third in 1960, but they slid to fifth in the middle of the 1961 season and finished sixth in 1962. The press and the fans wrung their hands, but the executives in the front office were hopeful. By 1963, general manager Bing

Devine had put in place some of the new players who would make the Cardinals the thoroughbreds of the National League. He had a new manager, too—Johnny Keane, a longtime toiler in the Cards organization who had served as a minor-league coach and manager. Keane, who had grown up in

Saint Louis and used to sneak into Sportsmans Park with his buddies to see games as a kid, fit right in. He knew baseball, and during his time in the minors he had learned that it was just as important to understand a player's emotions as it was to know his batting average. He arrived in 1963 to find a developing team that was on the brink

of something special and needed someone just like him to push them forward.

Bill White, who had broken in with the Giants and come to the Cardinals in 1959, was at first base. He produced right away, hitting .302 that year and making the All-Star team. He made it again in 1960, 1961, 1963 and 1964. He hit over .300

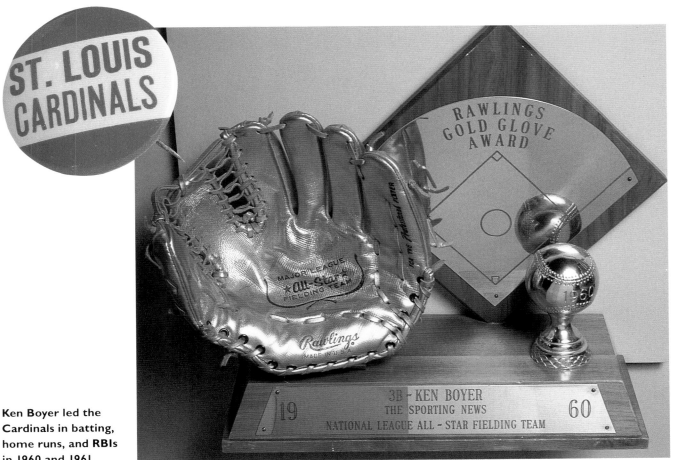

Ken Boyer led the Cardinals in batting, home runs, and RBIs in 1960 and 1961.

Bobbin' head dolls
became a collectible
hit in the 1960s.

ST. LOUIS

Tim McCarver is
well-known as a
broadcaster, but
Cardinals fans
remember him as
a steady player who
put in ten years
with the team.

SUNDAY NEWS
NEW YORK'S PICTURE NEWSPAPER

CARDS SWAT TIGERS
M'Carver, Cepeda HR in 7-3 Win

The Base Is Loaded

DAILY NEWS
NEW YORK'S PICTURE NEWSPAPER

FINAL

World Series Showdown:
GIBSON VS. McLAIN

Today, It's in Their Hands

ST. LOUIS CARDINALS
BOB
"THE GREAT"
GIBSON
NATIONAL LEAGUE CHAMPS

Bob Gibson was one of the game's top pitchers in the 1960s, winning game after game for the Cards and earning himself a niche in the Hall of Fame.

from 1962 through 1964. White, who later became a broadcaster and president of the National League, was also one of the major's top fielders, winning seven straight Gold Gloves at first base. By 1963, he was a seasoned veteran. Julian Javier was at second. Javier, a star product of the highly competitive baseball circuit in the Dominican Republic, Javier was obtained in a 1960 trade with the Pirates. Although an average hitter (.257 lifetime), he was one of the most talented second basemen in the league. General manager Bing Devine once said that Javier was better defensively than both Schoendienst and Rogers Hornsby. Javier played twelve years for the Cards.

Ken Boyer was at third. The amiable Boyer, a good fielder, was mysteriously sent to the outfield by Lane in 1957, where he floundered. Brought back to third in 1958 and made team captain, he responded by leading the team in batting, home runs, and RBIs in 1960 and 1961. By 1963 he was a grizzled veteran and team leader.

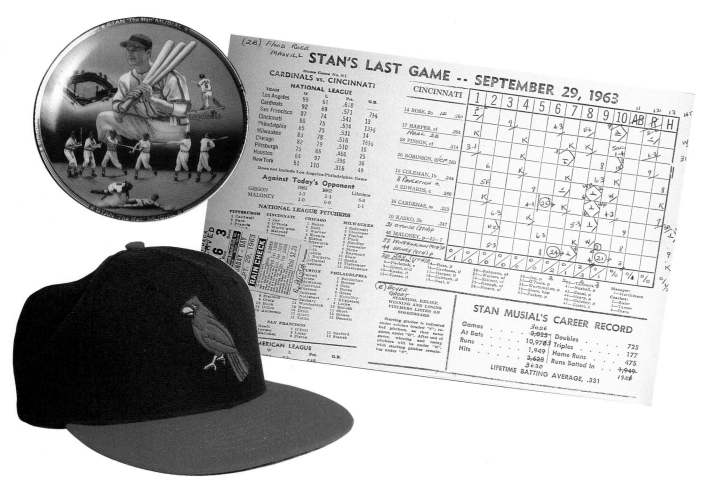

Even legends retire, and Stan the Man played his last game on September 29, 1963.

Curt Flood, who would make history in more ways than one, was in center field in the spring of 1963. He had arrived in 1958, after playing just eight games with the Reds, and started slowly. By 1961, though, he found his stroke. Curt hit .302 that year and followed it up with a .296 average in 1962. He was also becoming a fine center fielder, and his arrival enabled Boyer to go back to third. A 1963 trade brought

Dick Groat, the All-Star shortstop of the Pirates, to Saint Louis. An All-American at both baseball and basketball in college, Groat had been the hero of the World Series in 1960, after a super season with the Pirates in which he hit .325. Thinking he was over the hill, Pittsburgh traded him at the end of 1962, not knowing that he still had enough good years left to help the Cards win championships.

Tim McCarver, who broke into baseball at age seventeen, became the starting catcher in 1963 spring training after serving as a backup for three long years. And of course there was Bob Gibson. The pitcher, who almost died from a childhood illness, didn't know what he wanted to do as a teenager. A gifted athlete, he attended Creighton University in Omaha, Nebraska, on a basketball scholarship, even though he knew he was better at baseball. He loved basketball, though, and played a season with the clowns of the hardcourt, the Harlem Globetrotters. He finally wound up with the Cards in 1959 after playing minor-league ball in Omaha with Johnny Keane as his manager. Gibson did little in his first four years pitching for the Cards, winning thirty-four and losing thirty-six. Then his old boss Johnny Keane arrived as the Cards manager in 1961, giving him the confidence he needed. He won thirteen games that year and fifteen the next. In 1963, he would erupt, winning eighteen games.

That season was a watershed for the Cardinals. It was the final year for Stan

Lou Brock, here making his 893rd, record-breaking steal, came to the Cards in 1964 with little promise and took off, suddenly becoming a superstar.

Musial, who bowed out of baseball with a staggering 3,630 hits. But the Cards squad that would play together for the next half decade was coming together, and it was the first year since 1949 in which the Redbirds had a serious shot at the pennant. A 19–1 winning streak in July pulled them within a single game of the powerhouse

Dodgers, and they finished in second place, six games out. The season was a scintillating preview of what 1964 would bring.

The Cardinals, so good in 1963, stagnated in the spring of 1964. No one seemed to be able to spark a team that was, on paper, one of the best in years. In early June, the Cardinals were in seventh

The Cards rushed Bob Gibson after he struck out nine to win the 1964 World Series against the Yankees.

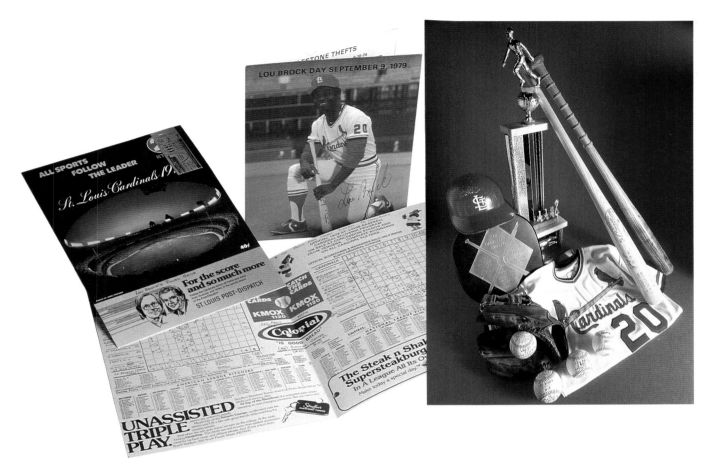

Lou Brock hit a sizzling .348 his first season with the Cards, and he never cooled down.

place. Determined to kickstart the ball club, Bing Devine and Johnny Keane brought infielder Mike Shannon and reliever Barney Schultz up from the minors. Then, on June 16, Devine made a bombshell trade—Ernie Broglio for Lou Brock. There was joy in Chicago. Ernie Broglio was one of the best pitchers in the National League, a veteran Saint Louis hurler who won twenty-one games in 1960 and eighteen in 1963. He had matu-

rity, poise, a wide array of pitches and confidence. There was sorrow in Saint Louis. They got a nobody. Lou Brock hit just .263 and .258 in his first two seasons with the Cubs, and although he was supposed to be a speedster, he managed to steal only sixteen bases in 1962 and twenty-four in 1963. He was inexperienced, an unproven fielder, and did not yet know the National League pitchers.

What happened to Lou Brock when

Memorabilia of a hero: news of Lou Brock's induction into the Hall of Fame, his 893rd stolen base, and the shoes that shod his fleet feet.

The Cardinals were tough in many different ways. As a pitcher, my biggest problems were always Lou Brock and Curt Flood, the two fastest men in baseball. They could steal, go to third on a single, score from second on an outfield hit. That was a danger to me as a pitcher I just didn't face with any other team.

—GAYLORD PERRY

94

Ken Boyer hit .287 lifetime and was one of the most popular players in Cards history.

in the Cards pennant chase. He began battering pitchers right away and tore up the National League, hitting a sizzling .348 for the Cards. He proved his speed, too, stealing thirty-three bases in 103 games. (Broglio had a dismal 4–7 record for Chicago that year, won just ten games in the next three years, and was let go.) The Cards, led by Brock, surged in August, moving up steadily in the rankings. Ken Boyer won the MVP award that summer, hitting .295, with twenty-four homers and 119 RBIs. Bill White hit .301 with twenty-one homers and 102 RBIs. Bob Gibson won nineteen games and struck out 245 batters. Ray Sadecki, a twenty-three-year-old pitcher, won twenty games. Still, with two weeks to go, the Cards were six games behind the Phillies. The Phillies, though, were in the middle of one of the great collapses of baseball history. They lost ten games in a row, as the Cards took nine of ten and their first pennant in eighteen years.

The prize, however, was the opportunity to face off in the World Series against the formidable New York Yankees —Whitey Ford, Mickey Mantle, Roger Maris, and the wonder infield of Clete Boyer (the brother of the Cards' Ken Boyer), Bobby Richardson, Tony Kubek, and Joe Pepitone. The Cards, out of World Series action for so long, did not dwell on

he unpacked his bags in Saint Louis remains one of the great mysteries of the ages. Did he find a rabbit's foot at Union Station? The unproven outfielder turned into a sudden superstar and was the driving force

game one, 9–5. The Cards were down 4–2 at one point, but came back strong with four runs in the sixth inning. The Bronx Bombers bounced back to win game two, 8–3, scoring four runs in the ninth after Bob Gibson was taken out. A Mantle homer in the ninth inning of game three brought the Yanks victory and a 2–1 margin. They built a 3–0 lead going into the sixth inning of game four, and it looked as though they would soon have a commanding three-games-to-one lead. Then, the Cards loaded the bases and Ken Boyer hit a grand slam. He trotted past his brother Clete, playing third base, with a wide smile on his face. Relief pitchers Roger Craig and Ron Taylor held the Yanks in check and the Cards won 4–3. The Cards took game five, 5–2, when McCarver, a power hitter who had played football in high school, hit a heroic home run in the tenth inning. Game six brought just what Saint Louis fans feared—the home-run hitting power for which the Yankees were so famous. Mickey Mantle and Roger Maris hit back-to-back home runs, then Joe Pepitone hit a grand slam as the Yanks tied the Series at three games each with the 8–3 win, setting up the climactic seventh game. Bob Gibson pitched brilliantly into the sixth inning and had plenty of support as the Cards built a 6–0 lead. Saint Louis fans had begun to cele-

Curt Flood's landmark lawsuit won free agency for players, and he was a fine player, too, hitting .293 lifetime.

how the Yanks had been dominating October since 1947. They just concentrated on playing hard baseball (some levity came from cut-up Bob Uecker, who practiced catching fly balls in batting practice before game one with a borrowed tuba). Ray Sadecki, hot from winning his twentieth game the week before, beat the Yanks in

brate when the Yankees switched on their power. Mantle hit a three-run homer, then two more Yank homers reduced the Cards' lead to 7–3 going into the ninth. Gibson yielded two more homers and got two batters out, but then up came Bobby Richardson, who had a record thirteen hits in the series. Fans held their breaths. All eyes were on the dugout, where coach Johnny Keane was expected to yank Gibson for a reliever. Keane, who had supreme confidence in Gibson, never budged from his seat. Gibson got the lethal Richardson to pop out to second, and the Cardinals had their first world championship since 1946.

Fans were in awe of Gibson. "He had a killer instinct. Every single batter was a war to him," remembers lifelong Cards fan Betty Doyle. "I sat right behind home plate during that Series, and I could see his face. He wanted to strike out every batter in that Series. He was a machine, a smooth-running machine."

It was the start of a seven-year stretch in which the Cards would win three pennants and two world championships, but it was a decade of turbulence, too. Not long before the 1964 Series, Busch had fired Bing Devine, the general manager. The day after the Series, in an

Ken Boyer's uniform anchors a display of his memorabilia in the Cardinals Hall of Fame.

Saint Petersburg, Florida, presented this trophy to their winter heros.

The Cardinals practice at Yankee stadium during the 1964 World Series.

announcement that stunned baseball fans from coast to coast, Cards world-champion manager Johnny Keane suddenly quit. Yankee skipper Yogi Berra was fired that same day, and the next day Keane was hired as the manager of the Yankees. Busch, who had talked to Leo Durocher about managing the team even while Keane was winning the World Series for him, came under pressure from the press and fans

not to sign Durocher. He turned instead to a fan favorite, former second baseman Red Schoendienst, and installed him as skipper. The redhead, who was to become one of the great Cards' managers, was uneasy that first season. He started the year badly, was in last place in just a few weeks, and never recovered, finishing seventh. Bob Gibson won twenty games, but the rest of the pitching staff faltered. The hitters fell into a season-long slump. New general manager Bob Howsam, looking to do something, traded away Bill White and Ken Boyer (who would die of cancer at fifty-one), then unloaded Bob Uecker and Dick Groat. Fans fumed. New players, among them Orlando Cepeda, Charley Smith, and Al Jackson, seemed to arrive daily. The trades did little good, though, and the Cards finished sixth in 1966.

The players were there, though. The Cards just needed to gel and to get lucky. In 1967, they did. Starting off with strong pitching, the Cards roared. Orlando Cepeda became the unquestioned team leader and led with his bat, hitting .325 with twenty-five home runs. Julian Javier had his best season, hitting .281. Brock hit .299 and continued to rip up the base paths, stealing fifty-two bases. (He had stolen 137 in the previous two years.) Curt Flood, who quietly became one of the top hitters in the league, hit .335. Roger Maris, who joined the team that year, hit .261 with fifty-five RBIs and played a superb right field. The pitching was good

A ball commemorates another world championship for the Cards, this one in 1967.

Red Schoendienst was one of baseball's finest second basemen, manning the bag for sixteen years with the Cardinals.

despite the six-week, midseason loss of Gibson, when a Roberto Clemente line-drive hit him. Two young pitchers, Nellie Briles and Steve Carlton, filled in for him, each winning fourteen games for the season. Dick Hughes, up from ten years in the minors, had a career year, winning sixteen games. On one tear, the Cards won twenty-one of twenty-five games, and on another, later in the year, took thirteen of fifteen. They were better as the season rolled on and won 101 games, taking the flag by ten and a half games.

This time, in the World Series they met the hard-luck Red Sox, who had struggled to win their pennant in the last week of the season. The tired Sox held the Cards pretty even in game one, but the Redbirds, with four hits by Brock, won 2–1 as Maris drove in the winning run. The Sox bounced back to take game two, 5–0, on a shutout by Jim Lonborg. Things started looking up after that as the Series came to Saint Louis and Nellie Briles won game three, 5–2, and Gibson took game four, 6–0. The Sox had Lonborg, though, who was at his peak in his very best year. He mixed up his pitches nicely, had good location on just about everything he threw, and beat the Cards, 3–1.

The Series returned to Boston and, buoyed by their cheering fans, the Sox

Saint Louis had reason to celebrate again in 1967.

A collection of pins ballyhoos several decades of fine baseball.

took game six, 8–4. Lonborg, the old workhorse, was asked to pitch the seventh game on just two days' rest and was weary. The Cards chipped away for two runs in the third, two in the fifth, and three in the sixth on their way to a 7–2 win and another world championship. The title solidified the Cards' position on top of the National League and established Lou Brock (who hit .414) and Bob Gibson (who pitched three complete games) as genuine superstars.

Gibson was good in 1967, but he was even better the next summer. In 1968 he posted an incredible 1.12 ERA, one of the lowest in history, pitched twenty-eight complete games in thirty-four starts, struck out 268, and threw thirteen shutouts. In midseason he won fifteen straight games and had forty-eight consecutive scoreless innings. He won the Cy Young Award and the MVP, winning twenty-two games. Fans look back and wonder how he ever lost nine games that summer. What separated Gibson from other good pitchers, players say, was his ability to concentrate and stay focused, no matter what was going on. He also pitched quickly and pitched his own game. He had no use for conferences with managers, coaches, and catchers, and waved them away when they approached. He knew what he wanted to do and did it. "I knew the batters, I knew the situations, inning by inning," he says. "Why slow things up with conferences and small talk? The faster I worked, the better I pitched."

Everything went right for the Cards in 1968, despite an anemic lineup in which only one batter, Curt Flood, hit over .300 and nobody hit more than sixteen home runs. Manager Red Schoendienst didn't need a lot of runs with the pitching he had, though. Bob Gibson was not the only ace

on the 1968 staff. That summer Nellie Briles had a 19–11 record, Steve Carlton went 13–11, and Ray Washburn was 14–8. Everything seemed to go right, even when things went wrong. For example, in one late-season series against the Giants, Gaylord Perry pitched a no-hitter against the Cards in a night game, and the next day, Ray Washburn pitched a no-hitter against the Giants. Pitching feats like these won the pennant for the Cardinals.

In the World Series, the Cards faced the streaking Detroit Tigers, whose Denny McLain had won thirty-one games that year. Bob Gibson let McLain know who

Bob Gibson struck out seventeen batters in game one of the 1968 World Series, setting a Series record.

It wasn't easy to decide who to include on this plaque.

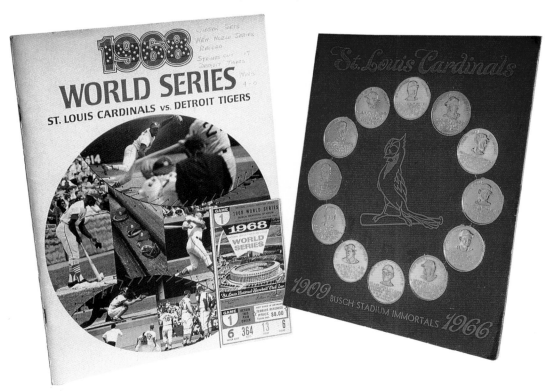

102

MUSIAL'S 1857 EXTRA BASE HIT SURPASSING BABE RUTH FOR MAJOR LEAGUE RECORD (HR)

Fitting mementoes of the 1960s—the Cards' latest home and a scorecard from the game in which Stan Musial broke Babe Ruth's extra-base record.

was king of the hill in game one, when they faced each other and Gibson won, 4–0, on a five-hit shutout and struck out seventeen in a row, a record. Fans hoped for a sweep, but it turned out to be a hard and heart-breaking Series for the Cardinals.

On the arm of Mickey Lolich, Detroit won game two, 8–1. The Cards roared right back, with Ray Washburn pitching, to take game three, 7–3. In game four, Gibson returned to the mound and not only beat Detroit 10–1, but hit a home run. Detroit would not quit, though, and won the next one, 5–3, again with Lolich, and took the Series home, one game back. Home was where the heart was, and the bats. The Tiger sluggers unleashed a terrifying assault in game six, getting ten runs in the third inning and going on to a lopsided 13–1 vic-

tory. In game seven, with Gibson facing Lolich, Curt Flood misplayed a never-to-be-forgotten line-drive that rolled to the fence for a triple. Detroit then scored three runs. They added another and won the game, 4–1, taking the Series.

The Cards, unable to keep up with the white-hot Miracle Mets and Cubs in 1969, dropped to fourth, traded Orlando Cepeda, and ended the decade in a tailspin. The team had nothing to be ashamed of, though. The Cards had ridden a comet in the 1960s, with two world championships, three pennants, and one second-place finish. Fans savored the memories, too, because the 1970s would bring lawsuits, trades, and turmoil. Another flag would not fly over Busch Stadium for nearly a generation.

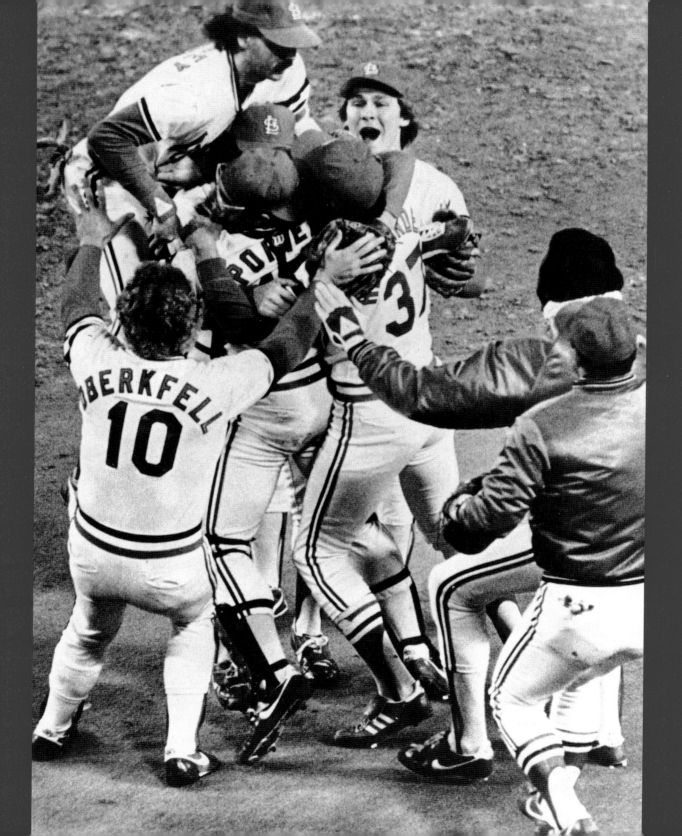

THE WIZARD, THE WHITE RAT, AND THE FUTURE

1970–1994

The pitcher glanced at Lou Brock on first, then at the plate, then back at Brock, then back to the plate, and began his wind-up. As soon as he did, Brock, Mercury in a baseball uniform, was off. As always, he went into his slide at exactly the right moment. A huge cloud of dirt and dust flew up as Brock's spikes hit the bag and the thud of a baseball filled the air. The umpire signaled safe, and the crowd stood and roared its approval. Lou Brock, who was having a super season in the summer of 1974, had just stolen his 118th base of the summer, setting a season record (later broken by Rickey Henderson), and batting .306. His averages for the first four years of the decade were .304, .313, .311, and .297. He hit .301 in 1975. The unproven player of 1965 had become a superstar.

The Brock story was typical of the Cardinals in the 1970s. Year after year, different Cardinals gave stirring performances, to the delight of the fans. Though they had no pennants to show for it, the Redbirds had teams loaded with stars. Saint Louis finished second three times in the 1970s (and came within a hair of winning the division title in 1974, finishing just half a game out).

Another fine player of the early 1970s was Joe Torre, who went on to a long career as a manager. He arrived in 1969 as a polished veteran after

Buried in the middle of the melee of exuberant Cards is pitcher Bruce Sutter, who saved the seventh and deciding game of the 1982 World Series against Milwaukee.

eight years with Milwaukee and Atlanta. He started off brilliantly, hitting .289 that first year, and then got better. Torre hit .325 in 1970 with 203 hits and 100 RBIs. The next season, 1971, was Joe Torre's year. Joe hit .363, and had 137 RBIs, 230 hits, and 352 total bases. He was the first player since Stan Musial in 1948 to lead the league in four categories. Torre went on to hit .289 in 1972, .287 in 1973, and .282 in 1974, when he was traded to New York.

Keith Hernandez came to Saint Louis in 1974 and in 1976 became the fulltime first baseman, hitting .289 that year. He was one of the Cards' most consistent hitters, with a .298 average for his sixteen-year career, and his defensive play made

him a star. He won eleven Gold Gloves, led the league in the number of double plays made by a first baseman six times, and led the league in assists by a first baseman five times. He rarely made errors. His combination of hitting and fielding won him an MVP award in 1979, when he hit .344 with forty-eight doubles and 111 RBIs.

Other fine Cardinals players of the 1970s were Jerry Mumphrey, Garry Templeton, Ted Simmons, Ted Sizemore, and Bake McBride. Bob Gibson started off the decade nicely, winning twenty-three games. He continued to pitch well into the 1970s, winning forty-seven more games over the next three years. His logical successor was Steve Carlton, who won fourteen games

Souvenirs took fans back to the good old days, but things were pretty swell in the 1970s. Joe Torre was the MVP in 1971, leading the league in four categories.

These matches were a fitting memento for the Cards in the 1970s—the team was hot.

Bob Forsch threw two no-hitters for the Cards.

in 1967, seventeen in 1969 (he started and won the All-Star game that year), and twenty in 1971. Carlton had a decent fastball and a dangerous curve that broke wide and down. In 1969 he developed an effective slider that gave him a formidable arsenal of pitches. By 1971 he was perhaps the best pitcher in baseball. Later in the decade, the Cards got excellent years from hurler Al Hrabosky.

Then there was Bob Forsch, a fine hurler who started out as a third baseman. Converted to a pitcher because of his strong arm. He seemed to have the magic touch for the most difficult task in all baseball, pitching the no-hitter. Forsch not only threw two of them in the minors, a remarkable feat in itself, but then threw two more for the Cards, in 1978, against the Phillies, and again in 1983, against the

107

The Cards traded pitcher Steve Carlton —who went on to become the first pitcher ever to win four Cy Young awards—after a salary squabble.

a 154–123 record over sixteen years, topped by his twenty-win season in 1977. Only Hall of Famers Bob Gibson and Jesse Haines won more games for the Cards than Forsch did.

Despite the good playing on the field, feuds and wars seemed to be never-ending for the Cards in the 1970s, in the dugout and in the front office. The most controversial event, and most publicized, was Curt Flood's landmark Supreme Court case against the Cardinals. On January 16, 1970, Flood filed suit against the team, charging that plans to trade him to Philadelphia violated antitrust laws. The suit challenged the writ of baseball's employment system, arguing that the legendary reserve clause, which bound players to their teams or required them to go where traded, was unconstitutional. Flood, who claimed that all ballplayers were slaves under the reserve clause, lost the case, but the publicity eventually led to free agency.

In another controversy, at the start of the decade pitcher Steve Carlton asked for a salary increase from $25,000 to $40,000. The team offered $31,000 and would go no higher. Carlton, holding out for more, missed part of spring training. He finally agreed to a two-year deal, but he and the team came to an impasse again in 1972. This time owner Auggie Busch became so

Expos. His brother Ken, who pitched for the Houston Astros, threw a no hitter in 1979, making the Forsches the first brothers ever to throw no-hitters in the majors. Bob Forsch was a reliable workhorse for the Cards in the 1970s and 1980s, posting

Pins are one kind of souvenir, but this autographed home plate, celebrating Glenn Brummer's steal that won a decisive game in the 1982 pennant race, is one of a kind.

fed up with the hurler that he traded him to Philadelphia. Angered and eager to get even, Carlton proceeded to have one of the greatest seasons in baseball history, winning twenty-seven games in 1972 for the Phillies and going on to win twenty games in a season five more times for them. It was the worst trade in Cardinal history. But a decade later, the Cards did it again, trading Keith Hernandez to the Mets when he was at his peak.

The Cards floundered through the end of the 1970s, hiring and firing managers. At one point the Cards brought back Ken Boyer, whom they had traded away in the 1960s, as manager, but they dumped him, too. The Cards weren't going anywhere in early 1980, either, but up in the front office, someone smelled a rat.

When sportscaster Bill Speith Dorrel first saw Norman Elvert Herzog play, he took a look at the player's thatch of eerily

CARDINALS FANS

Saint Louis was a baseball heaven in the 1930s, because you had not only the Browns and Cards but all the stars of both leagues coming to town. In a given week you'd see Gabby Hartnett, Pie Traynor, and Carl Hubbell from the National League and Babe Ruth, Lou Gehrig, Charlie Gehringer, and Jimmy Foxx from the American League. Why, if you went to Sportsman's Park every day for a week, you'd have the whole Hall of Fame playing in front of you.

—LOUIS COLUMBO, 80, SAINT LOUIS

The mascot charms his admirers.

Fans could buy pennants, coolers . . .

The Cardinals fans are very supportive. They're with you, win or lose. There's a lot of noise when you step into the batter's box make a good play. I remember in the middle of 1993 we went to Philadelphia and lost every game—knocked us right out of the race. When we came back the next day for a three-game series at Busch every single game was sold out. Where else do you see that kind of support? Nowhere.

—TODD ZEILE

The first year I started to go to games was 1930, the start of the Gashouse Gang era. They were real characters. They'd jump out of the dugout screaming when someone hit a single, like guys today for a grand slam. They were always playing pranks, arguing with umpires, cheering each other on. I think they played so well because they were so aggressive, but also because they genuinely liked each other. They wanted to see each other do well, and that's why the team did well.

—BETTE DOYLE, 70, FLORISSANT, MISSOURI

. . . hats . . . bowling pin–style statues . . .

. . . but someone couldn't resist "borrowing" this sign.

My big seller is Cardinals hats. My dad and I have been here selling hats for fifteen years and I think we've sold a Cardinals hat to every single kid in Missouri by now.

—CINDY VALENTINE, VENDOR, SAINT LOUIS

As the years go on, memorabilia becomes a part of everyday life, even showing up on the breakfast table.

Everybody complained about Sportsman's Park. It was old. It was rundown. It had Stone Age facilities. It was dirty. But it also had real charm, with the advertising signs and corners in the outfield fences. You were close to the field, too, part of the game. You just don't get that anywhere today. Give me old Sportsman's anytime.

—STEVE LOBSINGER, 46, FAIRVIEW HEIGHTS, ILLINOIS

These mugs could hold a lot of beer, and Auggie Busch had a lot of beer to fill them.

We had no major-league team in Muskogee, that's for sure. I had a Coke machine replica radio next to my bed. I'd listen to Harry Caray announce the Cards games every single night in the 1950s, until I fell asleep. The radio was off in the morning. I guess my mother turned it off. I know I wouldn't have.

—LARRY VAN BEBER, 41, MUSKOGEE, OKLAHOMA

Whitey Herzog and
Milwaukee skipper
Harvey Kuenn were
all smiles before the
1982 World Series.

The teams in the 1980s had hitting, pitching, speed, and determination. But that's not why we won. We won because of Whitey Herzog. He just seemed to know what was going to happen next, who would do what. He had an instinct, an intuition, I've never seen before.

—OZZIE SMITH

light blonde hair, almost snowy, and had a nickname for him—Whitey Herzog. Along the way, Herzog picked up another nickname: the *White Rat,* spoken affectionately, implying craftiness and invincibility. Players, media and fans picked it up quickly. Whitey Herzog went on to play for seven years in the minors and eight years in the majors, then became a Big League manager in 1973, with Texas. Later he managed the Kansas City Royals and brought them three straight division titles.

As Auggie Busch fumed with his Cardinals in Saint Louis, Herzog kept holding

up trophies in nearby Kansas City. He was fired in 1980 after some disputes with management, and Busch grabbed him, first naming him manager, then general manager. His orders were simple: Win. As soon as Herzog arrived in Saint Louis he told Busch that he could not win with the team. He needed a fast, bases-stealing, hit-and-run team for the large Busch Stadium field and, defensively, he needed a solid relief pitcher. Too many Cardinal victories died in late innings. Busch gave his new skipper carte blanche to do what he needed, and Herzog spent the rest of

Busch Stadium glows at night, and Auggie Busch himself, in bronze, welcomes visitors to the team's offices.

115

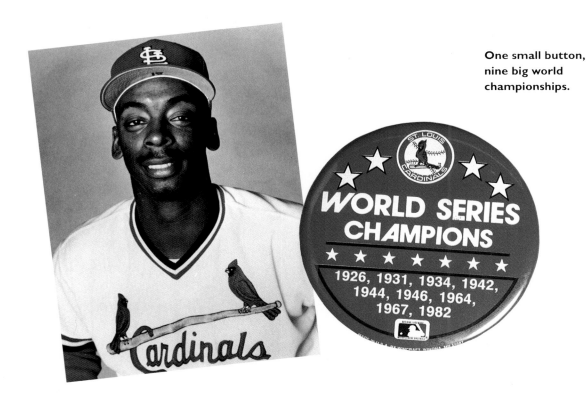

One small button, nine big world championships.

WORLD SERIES CHAMPIONS
1926, 1931, 1934, 1942, 1944, 1946, 1964, 1967, 1982

Two homers and two catches in game three made Willie McGee one of the heroes of the 1982 World Series.

1980 scouting talent throughout the country and left the managing to Red Schoendienst. When he was through, Herzog had made more trades than Marco Polo did when he first arrived in China with his European caravan.

His first move was to get a reliable catcher who could handle his current pitchers and the relievers he was scouting. He snared veteran Darrel Porter from Kansas City. Then he pulled off a huge, eleven-player trade with San Diego, landing Rollie Fingers, Bob Shirley, Gene Tenace, and Bob Geren. A day later he traded

Leon Durham, Ken Reitz, and Ty Waller to Chicago for ace reliever Bruce Sutter. Shortly after that, Ted Simmons let it be known he didn't want to play first, where Herzog wanted him, and demanded a trade. Whitey obliged, sending him and Rollie Fingers, who had not even unpacked yet, to Milwaukee with Pete Vuckovich to get Sixto Lezcano, Dave Green, Lary Sorensen, and Dave LaPoint. During the season, he unloaded pitcher Tony Scott to get Joaquin Andujar from Houston, and at the end of the season he landed Willie McGee in a trade with the Yankees.

Just before the start of the 1982 season, unable to get the four shortstops he wanted, Whitey "settled" for lightly regarded Oswald Smith of the Padres. In all, in just about a year, the White Rat unloaded fifteen players and added eleven. He completely rebuilt the St. Louis Cardinals, beginning a new era.

After a fourth-place finish in 1980, the Cards raced through the 1981 season with lots of hits, lots of runs, and lots of bad luck. They had a good ball club. Hitting was sound: Hernandez, .306; Templeton,

.288; Ken Oberkfell, .293; Dane Iorg, .327; and George Hendrick, .284. Bruce Sutter saved twenty-five games. Bob Forsch won twice as many games as he lost. But the 1981 season was shortened by a players' strike. By reshuffling schedules, the leagues managed to play a 102- to 110-game schedule (depending on the number of rainouts). In a decision straight out of a Marx Brothers movie, the commissioner's office decided to revamp the playoffs to pit the winners of each half of the season against each other for the pennant. This meant

These hats have been worn atop some mighty talented heads.

117

Herzog had another winning team in 1985, and the Cards went to the Series again.

ST. LOUIS CARDINALS
WHITEY HERZOG, MANAGER

that the Cardinals, who finished second in each half, were shut out of the playoffs. It was an infuriating situation and just made Herzog and the Cards want to win in 1982 that much more.

The team Whitey put on the field in 1982 was one of the finest in Saint Louis history, and it was a typical Herzog team. The players produced lots of wins, but few runs. There were lots of hits, but few home runs (George Hendrick led the team with just sixteen). Only one player had

more than 100 RBIs (Hendrick). Only one starter, Lonnie Smith, hit over .300. Yet the Cards won ninety games, took the division by three games, and swept Atlanta in the best-of-five league championship series. They did it with hit-and-run baseball, lots of steals, and a balanced pitching staff (Bob Forsch and Joaquin Andujar each won fifteen, Steve Mura won twelve, and three others won nine. Bruce Sutter had thirty-six saves).

Herzog looked forward to the Series.

Cards Coke bottles and Cards pillows (this one signed by the White Rat) join the retinue of memorabilia.

It was a chance to prove that his kind of fast baseball could take a team all the way to a world championship and a chance to win his own first Series ring. After game one, though, it looked like the only World Series memories for the Cards were still going to be old Stan Musial magazine covers. They were brutalized by the Milwaukee Brewers, losing 10–0. Herzog, intent on going with the men who did well all year, started raw rookie John Stuper in game two. Young Stuper pitched well and a sixth-inning triple by catcher Darrell Porter tied the game and the Cards went on to win, 5–4. The Cards won game

three, 6–2, with two homers by Willie McGee, who had only hit four homers all season. McGee also made two electrifying catches in the outfield, both depriving the Brewers of surefire homers. The Brewers bounced back to take the next two games, 7–5 and 6–4, and went back to Saint Louis with a three-games-to-two lead.

Herzog was so calm about the outcome of the Series that he spent the off-day before the final games fishing and ordered his players to spend the day relaxing, too. The strategy worked. The Cardinals, with rookie John Stuper again on the mound, crushed Milwaukee, 13–1,

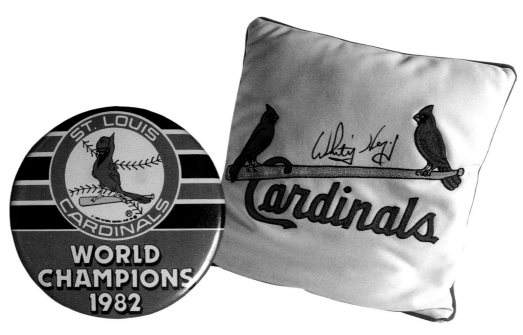

119

and then won the seventh game 6–3 to take the championship. Catcher Darrell Porter was the Series MVP.

Herzog was thrilled with the world championship for many reasons, but mostly because the win seemed to vindicate his style of baseball, the "run 'em into the ground" style that came to be known as "Whiteyball." In his autobiography, *White Rat*, Herzog wrote, "There were a lot of people around baseball who . . . said we didn't fit the mold, whatever that was, because Hendrick was the only guy in the lineup who could hit the ball out of the park with any regularity. They seemed to think there was something wrong with the way we played baseball, with speed and defense and line-drive hitters. If I have a motto, it's run, boys, run and I didn't see why we couldn't keep running for another couple of years."

The Cards slipped in 1983, finishing fourth, and were third in 1984, two-and-a-half games back. They lost reliever Bruce Sutter, who left as a free agent, and traded away Keith Hernandez to New York. The

Fans who followed the Cardinals through all the wins of the 1980s emerged from the decade laden with pins . . .

. . . and a battery of other mementoes.

pitching staff, so sharp in 1982, went south in 1983. The 1984 season was no better, but in 1985, things improved dramatically. By the middle of June, the Cards had obtained pitcher John Tudor, slugger Jack Clark, speed-demon Vince Coleman, pitcher Danny Cox, and center-fielder Andy Van Slyke and, late in the season, rookie reliever Todd Worrell and third-baseman Terry Pendleton.

In 1985, with a well balanced team on the field, Herzog had one of the best seasons in Cards history. Jack Clark came to town from San Francisco, where he had been one of the league's leading sluggers for nine seasons. He stepped right into the lineup in 1985 and hit .281 with twenty-two home runs and eighty-seven

RBIs. The big first baseman was hurt in 1986, but had a tremendous year in 1987, with a .286 average, thirty-five home runs, 106 RBIs, and a league-leading slugging average of .597. He left in 1988 after a contract squabble.

Tommy Herr was never a power hitter, but the vast outfields of Busch Stadium enabled him to place line-drive singles, much like the Cards hitters of the turn of the century. He had an innate ability to make contact with the ball, rarely striking out, and in 1985, batting third, he led the team in RBIs. He had a career high of 110 RBIs in 1985. Defensively, he was a superb second baseman and worked with Ozzie Smith to form one of the major's best double-play combinations. Willie

McGee, whom no one thought much of when he came to Saint Louis in the early 1980s, hit an average of .292 through the decade. He had a league-leading .353 average in 1985, the year he also had a league-leading 216 hits. Not only was he a good hitter, but he was also a fast and intelligent base runner and an adept base-stealer. He swiped twenty-four bases in 1982, then moved up to forty-three in 1984 and fifty-six in 1985.

The gem of the infield, though, was the Wizard of Oz, Ozzie Smith. He began to show promise as soon as he arrived in Saint Louis from San Diego in 1982, and he improved year after year. A .250 hitter in his first three seasons, he averaged .280

in the last four years of the 1980s. He was a fine stealer, swiping on average more than forty bases a year. Unquestionably, Smith was the finest shortstop in baseball in the 1980s and early 1990s. An acrobatic athlete, he would effortlessly dive for a throw and catch it barehanded. Fans eagerly awaited his trademark airborne somersaults. Smith led the league in assists seven times in the 1980s, tying a record, set a record for assists in a season (621), and led National League shortstops in putouts twice and in double players twice. The Cards rewarded Smith with a controversial $2.5 million in 1987, then baseball's highest salary.

Vince Coleman, the Florida Flash,

Ozzie Smith signed an envelope for a fan and his mug was plastered on a mug, but the best tribute of all to the acrobatic shortstop is this statuette showing him in action.

With his trademark somersaults, Ozzie Smith led the league in assists seven times in the 1980s; fans (and advertisers) loved him.

STARSHOTS 1991 MAJOR LEAGUE BASEBALL GREATS

OZZIE SMITH
Cardinals SHORTSTOP
149

		FIVE-YEAR PERFORMANCE PROFILE										
YR TEAM	BA	G	AB	H	R	2B	3B	HR	RBI	SB	BB	SO
86 Cardinals	.280	153	514	144	67	19	4	0	54	31	79	27
87 Cardinals	.303	158	600	182	104	40	4	0	75	43	89	36
88 Cardinals	.270	153	575	155	80	27	1	3	51	57	74	43
89 Cardinals	.273	155	593	162	82	30	8	2	50	29	55	37
90 Cardinals	.254	143	512	130	61	21	1		50	32	61	33
Career	.256	1926	7019	1798	.910	297	51	19	600	464	807	422

Born: December 26, 1954 Mobile, AL
Home: St. Louis, MO
Ht: 5'10" Wgt: 155 Bats: Switch Throws: Right

149

I never wanted the somersault to be a signature or anything. I just did it once in practice and the team's public relations director saw it and asked me to do it on fan appreciation day. I didn't think it was a big deal, but the people liked it, so I kept doing it. Some say I'll soon be too old to do it. Well, you just watch!

—OZZIE SMITH

The late, great
Red Schoendienst.

The Cards were
inducted into
the Hall of Fame
in 1989.

was a legend in the minors, where he led his league in stolen bases every single year, swiping an amazing 145 for Macon, Georgia, in 1983. He put all doubts about his ability to steal on major-league catchers to rest right away, stealing 110 bases in 1985, his first season with the Cards, just eight short of Lou Brock's old record. To let people know it was no fluke, he then stole 107 bases in 1986 and 109 in 1987, and he continued to lead the league in bases stolen each year. Coleman, who

not only admitted that he did not know which league the Cards were in when drafted and wasn't sure who Jackie Robinson was, either, became a stable hitter, too, to the surprise of management. He consistently batted around .270 during the decade and drew more than fifty walks a season. You can't steal bases if you don't get on, and Coleman always, somehow, got on.

John Tudor was an experienced pitcher who never quite realized his potential before arriving at Busch Stadium in 1985. He had a lackluster career with the Red Sox from 1979 to 1983, and he was just 12–11 with the Pirates in a single season there. At first, he proved the skeptics right, winning just one game in April and May and losing seven. Then, finding his rhythm, Tudor began to win and to win consistently. As the season wore on, he became a historical statistic, eventually winning twenty more games for a 21–8 record. Bad luck and injuries plagued him after that. He punched a ceiling fan after losing a World Series game in 1985 and badly cut his finger. He was injured in August of 1986 and missed the rest of the year. In 1987, in a macabre incident, Mets catcher Barry Lyons fell into the Cards dugout chasing a foul ball and landed on Tudor, breaking his leg.

The current crop of souvenirs, bound to be treasured collectibles within decades.

Busch Stadium set the standard for contemporary ballparks, and sparked a revitalization of downtown Saint Louis.

Like Tudor, the theatrical and loquacious Joaquin Andujar, perhaps the best pitcher to ever come out of the Dominican Republic, had no fan club when he arrived in Saint Louis. After all, he was just a .500 pitcher in six years with Houston (he claimed they couldn't handle his stylish demeanor) and, when traded to the Cards in 1981, he was just 2–3. He turned around quickly as soon as he walked into Busch Stadium, finishing with a smart 6–1 record and in 1981 then posting a 15–10 record in 1982 to help the Cardinals win the pennant, league championship, and World Series. He had a down year in 1983, finishing 6–16, but rebounded nicely in 1984 to win a league-leading twenty games. In 1985, he was invincible through the middle of August, winning twenty games and on the road to as many as thirty wins for the season. Then, he suddenly slumped badly and staggered to a 1–5 finish. Despite his fine year, he was traded to Oakland the next winter. Danny Cox was the rudder of the mound staff in the memorable 1985 season. He won eighteen and lost nine, but was usually close in defeat. Handcuffed by injuries, though, he pitched only three more seasons.

The Cardinals were super in 1985, but so were the New York Mets. The Cardinals went into August on a pace to win a hundred games, but they could not shake the Mets. Then . . . trouble. Jack Clark hurt his rib cage and was out of

action. Herzog went through his dog-eared sheaths of scouting reports and recruited lightly regarded Cesar Cedeno from the Reds. In the remaining twenty-eight games of the season Cedeno hit six home runs and drove in nineteen runs. Always in search of more bullpen help, on a hunch Herzog brought up tall, reed-thin reliever Todd Worrell from the Cardinals AAA club in Louisville. What a hunch! Worrell stepped right into the maelstrom of the pennant race and won three and saved five. During the final week of the season, the Cards dropped two key games to the Mets, allowing them to pull within a single

Commemorative baseballs are hot items at the souvenir stands at Busch Stadium, which glows during a game on a recent, hot summer night.

127

These items are soft, but they commemorate a hard-edged team.

Journeyman reliever Juan Agosto wore these shoes as he picked up his twenty-ninth career save in 1991.

game. It was crunch time. Danny Cox, old reliable, took the mound the night after the two loses and shut down the streaking Mets, 4–3. The Cards then went on to defeat the Cubs in two games and become the divisional champs.

The Redbirds went up against the blue machine of the Dodgers in the play-offs, which opened in Los Angeles. The Dodgers pounded the Cards in the first two games, 4–1 and 8–2. Back in Saint Louis, the Redbirds won game three, 4–2, on a home run by Tommy Herr. Just before game four, in a weird accident, grounds-crew workers rolled the tarpaulin over speedster Vince Coleman's leg, putting him

out of action. Miraculously, his replacement, Tito Landrum, put into the lineup with almost no notice, went four for five that day and led a Cardinal hit parade that produced twelve runs in a 12–2 route. The Cards won game five 3–2 when Ozzie Smith, never a power hitter, crashed a long, ninth-inning home run. When that happened, car horns all over Missouri began honking in joy. In game six it was another long homer, this one by Jack Clark, that brought another victory and the second trip to the World Series in just four years.

The Cards met the Kansas City Royals in the Series, the first all-Missouri match

One of the Cards' mementoes of glory.

WORLD CHAMPIONSHIP TROPHY
PRESENTED BY THE COMMISSIONER OF BASEBALL

since 1944, when the Cards and Browns, cotenants of Sportsman's Park, had faced off. The Cards won the opener, 3–1, then scored four runs in the ninth to win game two, 4–2, thanks to a double by Terry Pendleton. The Royals took game three behind Bret Saberhagen, 6–1, and the Cards jumped back to take the fourth game on a 3–0, five-hit shutout by John Tudor. The Royals won the next one to bring the Series back to Kansas City. There, Don Denkinger, who did not play for anybody but was the first-base umpire, managed to get more ink than all the players combined. The Cards led 1–0 in the ninth, just an inning away from the world championship. Jorge Orta hit a ground ball to second, and Tommy Herr stopped it and made a routine throw to Todd Worrell, covering first. Worrell stepped on the bag and smiled. He could almost feel the Series ring being slipped onto his finger. Denkinger, though, to the astonishment of even the Royals, called Orta safe and said Worrell missed the bag. Television networks broadcast the replay for weeks and Orta was clearly out (Denkinger later admitted his mistake). The Royals went on to win the game. The next day, totally demoralized, the Cards were clubbed, 11–0 and Herzog was ejected by the home plate umpire who was—who else?—Don Denkinger. Frustrated Cards fans knew they had been robbed.

The Cards celebrated their one-hundredth anniversary as a National League Team with these special souvenirs.

The Cards finished a lackluster third in 1986, well behind the sensational New York Mets, who went on to win the World Series. To get the magic back in 1987, the Cards traded Andy Van Slyke, Mike LaValliere, and pitcher Mike Dunne to the Pirates for catcher Tony Peña, who promptly broke his thumb and was out until the end of May, taking sick leave along with John Tudor, who broke his leg on April 19. Despite the loss of two key players for months, the Cards did well, holding their own through the spring and eking their way into first place in early June. They spent the rest of the summer fighting off Montreal, who finished third, and the dogged Mets, who always seemed to stand between the Cardinals and a playoff series. The annual battle with the Mets once again came down to the last week of the season, and once again the pitching staff saved the flag for the Cards. Holding a shaky two-game lead with seven games to play, the Cards shut out the Expos in a double-header and locked up first.

The playoffs against the hard-hitting Giants started tentatively. The Cards and Giants split the first two games, the Cards won game three, and the Giants took games four and five. It looked like they were a blade of grass away from elimination. Then the old reliables, the pitchers, moved in. John Tudor, Todd Worrell, and Ken Dayley got together for a six-hit shutout in game six, and Danny Cox shut out the Giants 6–0 in the seventh game to win the playoffs.

The World Series of 1987 will always be remembered as the "Hanky Series" or the "Hefty Bag Series" or the "Dome Series." In the first game the Minnesota Twins rocked the Cards, 10–2, in their dome at home, whose plastic walls looks like the sides of a hefty bag. By the time the Series was over, the Twins had won four games in their dome, as thousands of fans waved white handkerchiefs to spur them on to slam homers. A sharp Cardinal team won the three games in Saint Louis, and almost pulled off the Series in the last game, staying ahead 2–1 into the fifth inning, when the Twins came back to win 4–2.

It was the last World Series of the 1980s for the Cards. They slipped to fifth place in 1988 and finished third in 1989, sixth in 1990, and second in 1991. Crafty,

The Cards have a long association with beer, but this pin links them with America's favorite soft drink.

This honor is borne of civic pride.

An impressionistic wooden sculpture and a library of books pay tribute to one of the game's greatest teams.

An invaluable member of the team keeps an eye on proceedings at Busch Stadium.

crusty old Auggie Busch, 90, a giant in American baseball, died in 1989. As the 1990s began, the Cards took the field with only a few players from the 1985 and 1987 pennant-winning teams. They struggled badly. They were in the National League East cellar at the All-Star break. Fed up and a little tired, Whitey Herzog suddenly resigned, ending a long and glorious era. He was replaced by an old fan favorite, Joe Torre, and under his guidance the Cards have rebounded. "The best manager is the guy who's been there, who's played the game, and that's Joe," says catcher Tom Pagnozzi. "He instills confidence in everybody."

As the Cardinals move toward the end of the century, they are, like the Yankees and Dodgers, one of the great teams of baseball, an institution as much as a team. Chris Von Der Ahe's amusements, Branch Rickey and his network of farm teams, Stan the Man and his lethal bat, the last hurrah of Pete Alexander, the antics of the Gashouse Gang, the Wizard of Oz and his acrobatic somersaults . . . this is the stuff of great baseball. And when the ballpark empties at night, listen closely. In the far reaches of the grandstands you can hear in a faint whisper that recognizable old Oklahoma twang. "Hell, me and Paul will win forty-five between us this summer. . . ."

CARDINALS GREATS

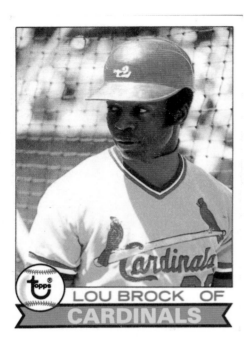

LOU BROCK

Lou Brock arrived in Saint Louis with an explosion in 1964. He hit .311, had two hundred hits, and stole forty-three bases in leading the Cards to a world championship. It was merely a sign of things to come. He would hit over .300 seven times in his sixteen years with the Cards, with 149 homers and 900 RBIs. He was a terror in October, too, just like Bob Gibson, hitting .391 with four homers in three World Series. But it was what Brock did once he got on base that made him a legend. Using speed, a large lead, and an uncanny sense of timing, he became the greatest base stealer of his time, shattering Ty Cobb's record with his total of 938 (later broken by Rickey Henderson). After his initial 43 thefts for the Cards in 1964, he stole 63 bases in 1965, 52 more in 1967, 62 in 1968, and an electrifying 118 in 1974 (he still holds the World Series record of 14 steals). He was enshrined at Cooperstown in 1985.

CURT FLOOD

Ballplayers will remember Curt Flood forever, but not for his .293 lifetime batting average with the Cards, his .335 season in 1967, or his league-leading 211 hits in 1964. Flood, outraged that the Cards would trade him to Philadelphia after his twelve years of faithful service, took the team to court and challenged baseball's sacred reserve clause, which bound players to one team for life unless traded. He fought the reserve clause all the way to the U.S. Supreme Court and lost, but his legal battle opened the door for other suits that eventually resulted in free agency and today's multi-million dollar salaries. (Flood himself never made more than $110,000 a season).

BOB GIBSON

Whenever people who know great pitching get together to argue who was the best, someone is likely to mention the figure 1.12. That was Gibson's earned run average in his super season of 1968, when he compiled a 22–9 record (with thirteen shutouts), struck out 268 batters, led his team to the world championship, and won both the MVP and Cy Young Awards. It was one of many great years for the hurler, though. Overall, he won 251 and lost 174. He made the All- Star team seven times and won two Cy Youngs and eight Gold Gloves. It was his World Series pitching that made Gibson so memorable, however. In just three fall classics he won seven games and lost just two. Only Whitey Ford, who pitched in eleven World Series, won more. Gibson's 1.89 ERA in Series play was one of the lowest ever, and his records of seventeen strike-outs in one game and thirty-five in one Series still stand.

Gibson, who mixed fastballs, curves, and sliders and never relied on one pitch, was one of the game's most consistent hurlers, averaging nineteen wins a season from 1963 to 1972. He fanned more than two hundred batters in nine seasons, led the National League in shutouts four times, and pitched one no-hitter. He did all this in a career plagued by a fractured leg, strained ligaments, bad knees, and a broken leg. He was elected to the Hall of Fame in 1981.

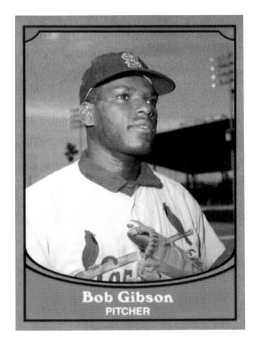

Bob Gibson
PITCHER

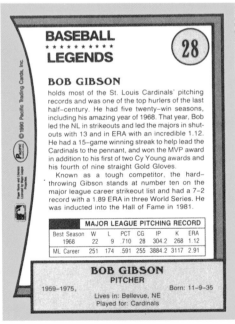

BASEBALL
★ ★ ★ ★ ★ ★ ★ ★ ★
LEGENDS

28

BOB GIBSON

holds most of the St. Louis Cardinals' pitching records and was one of the top hurlers of the last half–century. He had five twenty-win seasons, including his amazing year of 1968. That year, Bob led the NL in strikeouts and led the majors in shut-outs with 13 and in ERA with an incredible 1.12. He had a 15-game winning streak to help lead the Cardinals to the pennant, and won the MVP award in addition to his first of two Cy Young awards and his fourth of nine straight Gold Gloves.

Known as a tough competitor, the hard–throwing Gibson stands at number ten on the major league career strikeout list and had a 7–2 record with a 1.89 ERA in three World Series. He was inducted into the Hall of Fame in 1981.

MAJOR LEAGUE PITCHING RECORD							
	W	L	PCT	CG	IP	K	ERA
Best Season 1968	22	9	.710	28	304.2	268	1.12
ML Career	251	174	.591	255	3884.2	3117	2.91

BOB GIBSON
PITCHER

1959-1975,

Born: 11-9-35

Lives in: Bellevue, NE
Played for: Cardinals

WHITEY HERZOG

The "White Rat" was one of the great Cardinals managers of all time, bringing Saint Louis four pennants and a world championship during the 1980s. He was already a winner when he arrived in Saint Louis in 1980, having taken Kansas City to three straight divisional championships in 1976, 1977, and 1978. Whitey (nicknamed in the minors for his light blond hair) had the best record in the division in his first full year in Saint Louis, but did not make the playoffs in that season because of a players' strike and the playoff system that resulted (the first-half winner met the second- half winner, regardless of records). Whitey got even in 1982, though, blanking Atlanta (3–0) to take the pennant then beating Milwaukee for the world championship in seven games. He won pennants again in 1985 and 1987.

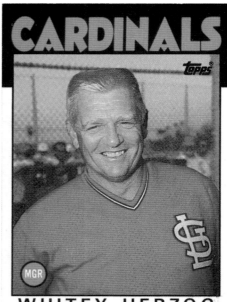

WHITEY HERZOG

ROGERS HORNSBY

The consummate hitter of his era, Hornsby adapted a stance that kept him back from the plate and deep in the batter's box, giving him an extra millisecond to watch the path of the ball. Using an incredibly level swing, he was able to hit to all fields with power. He hit .313 in his rookie year, 1916, with the Cardinals and .327 in his second. He slipped to .281 in his third season, the only full season he would hit below .30 in his career. He bounced back to .318 in 1919 and then went on a historic tear, hitting over .370 in each of the next six seasons, to lead the league in hitting. In three of those years he topped .400, with a high of .424 in 1924. Hornsby had a .358 lifetime average, the second- highest in major-league history, and led the Cards to a pennant in 1926.

He was such a good hitter that umps let him call his own pitches. Johnny Sain once threw three close pitches to Hornsby that "The Rajah" just watched go past him, and umpire Bill Klem called balls. Sain argued they should have been strikes. "Young man, when you pitch a strike, Mr. Hornsby will let you know," said the ump. Hornsby was, however, a blunt, irascible man (also a compulsive gambler), who annoyed players and owners alike. Despite his superhuman hitting he was traded away after the 1926 season, which infuriated Cardinals fans. He bounced to the New York Giants, then the Boston Braves and the Chicago Cubs as player-manager. He never failed in the batter's box, hitting .387 for Boston in 1928 and .380 for Chicago in 1929, but he never won in the clubhouse, turning off just about everyone he came in contact with—the Cubs hated him so much they refused to vote him a World Series share in 1932, even though he was manager during half the season. He was enshrined in the Hall of Fame in 1942.

JOE MEDWICK

DUCKY MEDWICK

Joseph Medwick was quickly nicknamed Ducky for his waddling walk. He came to the Cards in 1932, just as the infamous Gashouse Gang was forming. Medwick, with his walk and his own affinity for zaniness, was a charter member. He was legendary for his Gashouse Gang antics and for having been showered with bottles in the 1934 World Series; that notoriety overshadowed his sensational statistics, which got him into the Hall of Fame in 1968.

Ducky, MVP in 1937, hit .324 lifetime, with 205 homers and 1,383 RBIs. He hit a staggering .349 as a rookie, hit .300 during his first eleven seasons, and drove in 100 RBIs six consecutive years. He led the league in both RBIs and doubles three years (1936, 1937, and 1938), hit forty or more doubles seven years in a row, and in 1937 won the Triple Crown, with thirty-one homers, 154 RBIs, and a .374 average. He was later traded to the Brooklyn Dodgers, and his career ended shortly thereafter.

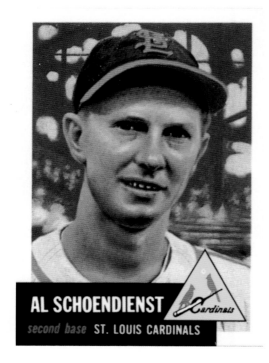

AL SCHOENDIENST *Cardinals*
second base ST. LOUIS CARDINALS

RED SCHOENDIENST

It is remarkable that this legendary infielder even played baseball. He talked his way into the army during World War II, despite a severe eye injury that would have kept most men out. Discharged from the army because of multiple wartime injuries, he then talked his way into the Cardinals lineup in 1945. With a .289 lifetime average, Red was second in National League hitting in 1953 with a .342 mark. As a fielder he had few equals. His 1956 fielding record of .9934 at second base remained unbroken for thirty years. Schoendienst was traded in 1956, and in 1958 he helped the Braves to a pennant, even though he played all year with bruised ribs, a broken finger, and pleurisy. He contracted tuberculosis in 1959, and lost part of a lung to it, but made a remarkable comeback with the Cards in 1961 and 1962. The tough-skinned Schoendienst, always popular with fans, became the Cards' skipper in 1965 and held the job for twelve years, winning pennants in 1967 and 1968 and the world title in 1968. He was elected to the Hall of Fame in 1992.

BIBLIOGRAPHY

Fleming, G. H. *The Dizziest Season*. New York: William Morrow, 1984.

Gregory, Robert. *Diz*. New York: Viking, 1992.

Holway, John. *Blackball Stars*. Westport, Conn.: Meckler Books, 1988.

Lieb, Frederick. *The St. Louis Cardinals*. New York: G. P. Putnam's Sons, 1944.

Petersen, Robert. *Only the Ball Was White*. Englewood Cliffs, N.J.: Prentice-Hall, 1970.

Rains, Rob. *St. Louis Cardinals*. New York: Saint Martin's Press, 1992.

Shatzkin, Mike. *The Ballplayers*. New York: William Morrow, 1990.

Tiemann, Robert. *Cardinal Classic*. St. Louis: Baseball Histories, Inc., 1982.

Wolff, Rick, ed. *The Encyclopedia of Baseball*. New York: Macmillan, 1990.

CARDINALS STATS

CARDINALS ALL-TIME PITCHING LEADERS

GAMES

Haines	554
Gibson	528
Sherdel	465
Forsch	455
Brazle	441
Doak	376
McDaniel	336
Jackson	330
Hrabosky	329
Sallee	316

SHUTOUTS

Gibson	56
Doak	32
Cooper	28
Brecheen	25
Haines	24
Dean	23
Lanier	20
Pollet	20
Forsch	19
Broglio	18

INNINGS PITCHED

Gibson	3885
Haines	3204
Forsch	2658
Sherdel	2450
Doak	2387

Sallee	1902
Breitenstein	1897
Brecheen	1790
Dean	1736
Jackson	1672

EARNED RUN AVERAGE

Tudor	2.52
Sallee	2.67
Taylor	2.67
Lush	2.74
Ames	2.74
Cooper	2.77
Beebe	2.79
Lanier	2.84
Brecheen	2.91
Gibson	2.91

WINS

Gibson	251
Haines	210
Forsch	163
Sherdel	153
Doak	145
Dean	134
Brecheen	127
Cooper	105
Sallee	105
Lanier	101
Jackson	101

WINNING PERCENTAGE

Tudor	.705
Cooper	.677
Dean	.641
Warneke	.629
Alexander	.618
Brecheen	.617
Brazle	.602
Munger	.602
Pollet	.599
Lanier	.594

COMPLETE GAMES

Gibson	255
Haines	209
Breitenstein	196
Sherdel	144
Doak	144
Dean	141
Sallee	122
Brecheen	122
Cooper	105
Powell	101

STRIKEOUTS

Gibson	3117
Dean	1087
Forsch	1079
Haines	979
Carlton	951
Doak	938
Jackson	899
Brecheen	857
Bend Mizell	789
Hallahan	784

SAVES

Worrell	129
Sutter	127
Smith	117
McDaniel	64
Hoemer	60
Brazle	60
Hrabosky	59
Dayley	39
Dean	30
Wilks	29

CARDINALS ALL-TIME BATTING LEADERS

BATTING AVERAGE

Hornsby .... .359
Mize .... .336
Medwick .... .335
Musial .... .331
Hafey .... .326
Bottomley .... .325
Frisch .... .312
Watkins .... .309
Torre .... .308
Collins .... .307

GAMES

Musial 3026
Brock 2289
Slaughter 1820
Schoendienst 1795
Flood 1738
Boyer 1667
Smith 1625
Hornsby 1580
Javier 1578
Simmons 1564

DOUBLES

Musial 725
Brock 434
Medwick 377
Hornsby 367
Slaughter 366
Schoendienst 352

Bottomley 344
Simmons 332
Frisch 286
Smith 283

AT-BATS

Musial 10972
Brock 9125
Schoendienst 6841
Slaughter 6775
Boyer 6334
Flood 6318
Hornsby 5881
Smith 5851
Simmons 5725
Javier 5631

TRIPLES

Musial 177
Hornsby 143
Slaughter 135
Brock 121
Bottomley 119
Konetchy 93
Medwick 81
McGee 76
Martin 75
Templeton 69

RUNS

Musial 1949
Brock 1427
Hornsby 1089
Slaughter 1071
Schoendienst 1025
Boyer 988
Bottomley 921
Flood 845
Frisch 831
Smith 813

HOME RUNS

Musial 475
Boyer 255
Hornsby 193
Bottomley 181
Simmons 172
Mize 158
Medwick 152
Slaughter 146
White 140
Brock 129

HITS

Musial 3630
Brock 2713
Hornsby 2110
Slaughter 2064
Schoendienst 1980
Boyer 1855
Flood 1853

Bottomley 1727
Simmons 1704
Smith 1592

RUNS BATTED IN

Musial 1951
Slaughter 1148
Bottomley 1105
Hornsby 1072
Boyer 1001
Simmons 929
Medwick 823
Brock 814
Frisch 720
Mize 653

STOLEN BASES

Brock 888
Coleman 549
Smith 395
McGee 274
Smith 203
Frisch 195
Huggins 174
Smith 173
Herr 152
Konetchy 151

INDEX

PHOTOGRAPHY CREDITS